The Twelve of England

Deeds of Arms Series

Series Editor: Steven Muhlberger, Nipissing University

This series of source readers makes available to a broad audience original accounts of famous displays of martial and chivalric prowess from the Middle Ages and early Renaissance. The books provide short, vivid introductions to particular topics and events, and can also be used in combination to look at the complex phenomenon of chivalric competition. Each volume includes a comprehensive introduction, color gallery of contemporary illustrations, and bibliography for further reading. Five volumes are currently scheduled for publication; others are under consideration.

Check our website for updates: www.freelanceacademypress.com.

DEEDS OF ARMS SERIES VOLUME 3

The Twelve of England

Translated and Edited by Noel Fallows

Freelance Academy Press, Inc.
www.FreelanceAcademyPress.com

Cover Illustration: The Battle of Aljubarrota, August 14, 1385, showing the armies of King Juan I of Castile (viewer's left) and King João I of Portugal (right). From Jean de Wavrin, Seigneur de Forestel, *Les Chroniques d'Angleterre,* late fifteenth century. London, British Library, Ms. Royal 14.E.IV, fol. 204r. Copyright © British Library Board. All Rights Reserved.

Freelance Academy Press, Inc., Wheaton, IL 60189
www.freelanceacademypress.com

Printed in the United States of America
by Publishers' Graphics

22 21 20 19 18 17 16 15 14 13 1 2 3 4 5

ISBN 978-1-937439-04-0

Library of Congress Control Number: 2013908141

Contents

List of Illustrations

Foreword

The Twelve of England

Tales of deeds of arms played an important role in the culture, politics, and warfare of the Middle Ages and the Renaissance. This series aims to make available in modern English historical sources—factual and fictional—describing chivalric accomplishment and aspiration, sources which have been in most cases entirely inaccessible.

The Twelve of England is a worthy addition to this project, since it opens the door to Portuguese chivalry. Portugal, like the other kingdoms of the Iberian peninsula, was pulled into the Hundred Years War and some of the most famous episodes of its military history took place in connection with that great conflict. The war in turn generated chivalric deeds and chivalric legendry famous in Portugal but unfortunately obscure elsewhere.

This series is proud to present to an English-speaking audience the iconic Portuguese tale known as the "Twelve of England." We are especially happy to have as our guide the leading expert on late medieval Iberian chivalry, Dr. Noel Fallows, author of the encyclopedic *Jousting in Medieval and Renaissance Iberia*.

Steven Muhlberger
Series Editor
Nipissing University

Preface

A short monograph demands a short Preface, so I shall focus primarily on thanking those who have helped bring this project to fruition. Firstly, I am indebted to my friend and colleague Dr. Amélia Hutchinson in the Department of Romance Languages at the University of Georgia for allowing me access to her impressive personal library of Portuguese books. In a similar spirit of generosity my colleague Dr. Robert Moser, also in the Department of Romance Languages at UGA, read through an early draft of the translation and made several helpful suggestions for improvement. Dr. Tobias Capwell at the Wallace Collection in London helped me resolve some of the knotty weaponry issues that have stumped previous editors of the text. The editors of the Deeds of Arms Series, Mr. Gregory Mele and Dr. Steven Muhlberger, also cast a critical eye over my manuscript and made constructive comments that I have taken into account. It goes without saying that any errors or misunderstandings that remain are my responsibility alone.

Much of the research for this book was conducted at the Wallace Collection and the British Library in London. It would be remiss of me not to express my gratitude to Alan T. Dorsey, Dean of the Franklin College of Arts and Sciences at UGA, who provides me with a research account in my role as Associate Dean which allows for travel to the museums and archives that make publications such as this possible.

Finally, I should also mention here that in order to avoid confusion I refer to the principal characters in the text by their proper names in the appropriate form for the language that they spoke. This struck me as a particularly necessary step when differentiating between the three "Johns": John of Gaunt; King Juan I of Castile; and King João I of Portugal.

PROF. NOEL FALLOWS FSA
University of Georgia

1. Introduction

Text and Context

The "Twelve of England" are in reality twelve intrepid, border-crossing Portuguese knights who prove their mettle by performing chivalric deeds of arms in England, and subsequently in other parts of continental Europe. Their legendary deeds might best be described as a medieval Portuguese version of Hollywood hype—a series of plausible yet fictitious deeds of arms framed within a much broader and sweeping historical context; a winning formula that has survived to the modern era in novels, movies, and mini-series. From a modern point of view the text edited in the present volume which describes these events is, like a mini-series, episodic in structure; and from a medieval point of view it is analogous to a triptych, with three distinct parts, each interconnected by the principal characters and some common linguistic threads. Holistically, this text epitomizes what Jesús D. Rodríguez-Velasco describes as "the chivalric fable,"[1] that is, the kaleidoscopic fusion of fantasy and reality that informs and shapes the tensions, paradoxes and contradictions of chivalric discourse and culture throughout the Middle Ages, and that even defines the concept of Chivalry itself.

---

1 Rodríguez-Velasco, *Order and Chivalry*, pp. 5–8.

As noted by Carlos Guilherme Riley, the Portuguese knights do not operate in the text within Portugal or even the Iberian peninsula, but within a geographic triangle defined by the principal trade routes associated with Portugal: England, Burgundy, and France.[2] Of the twelve, only a handful are named, and the text focuses on stories about the deeds of Álvaro Gonçalves Coutinho in the first and third sections, and a story about Álvaro Vasques de Almada in the second section, which corresponds to the central panel of the triptych.

The *Deeds of the Twelve of England* are well known in the Portuguese-speaking world due to the fact that the great Portuguese poet Luis Vaz de Camões (ca. 1524–80) included a highly stylized version of the tale in his epic poem and masterpiece *The Lusíads*, first published in 1572, in which he explicitly compares the Twelve of England to the legendary Twelve Peers of Charlemagne.[3] It is fair to say that Camões is as iconic a poet in the Portuguese-speaking world as Shakespeare is in the English-speaking world, such is his importance in the Portuguese (and world) literary canon. However, although Camões' version of the tale is the best known, it is not the first. The story in its earliest known written iteration has received very little attention, and is known only to a handful of specialists. It is included at the end of a manuscript copy of an extensive chronicle by Fernão Lopes (ca. 1385–after 1459) about the reign of King João I of Portugal: Ms. 87 of the Biblioteca Pública Municipal of Porto. This manuscript is written in a sixteenth-century cursive hand and dates to around 1550.[4]

In so far as the setting of the *Deeds of the Twelve of England* is concerned, the first clue is the anonymous author's mention of "the Battle." This reference is of particular importance for the original date of the text. It may seem cryptic now, but obviously was not when the text was originally composed. It is akin to

---

2 Riley, *Os Doze de Inglaterra: Ficção e Realidade*, p. 49.

3 In English, see Camões, *The Lusíads*, trans. White, Canto VI, stanzas 42–69, pp. 127–32. Camões makes the comparison to the Twelve Peers of Charlemagne in Canto I, stanza 12, p. 5.

4 On the date of the manuscript see Magalhães Basto, *O essencial sobre Os Doze de Inglaterra*, p. 5; and Riley, *Os Doze de Inglaterra: Ficção e Realidade*, p. 25. The manuscript is described in detail in the online resource *BITAGAP*, Manid. 1366.

referencing the Second World War in our own times simply as "the War." The reference to "the Battle" points to a battle of monumental importance to the history of Portugal that had taken place in living memory, namely, the battle of Aljubarrota (August 14, 1385).[5] At this battle the forces of twenty-eight-year-old King João I of Portugal (1357–1433; ruled 1385–1433; fig. 1, p. 45) won a decisive victory over the Castilian army of King Juan I of Castile (1358–90; ruled 1379–90). In a dramatic fifteenth-century depiction of this battle in fig. 2 (p. 46), King João has dismounted and is participating in the fray, cutting into the neck of his latest victim. The battle of Aljubarrota stopped the Castilian invasion of Portugal dead in its tracks, and was an important catalyst for a strategic alliance between Portugal and England, as well as Portuguese independence, about which there is more below.

Another important battle in the history of medieval Portugal is mentioned in the text in connection with the death of Álvaro Vasques de Almada: the battle of Alfarrobeira. The Alfarrobeira is a stream located about 20 miles north of Lisbon. At the battle of Alfarrobeira, which took place on May 20, 1449, the forces of King Afonso V of Portugal (1432–81; ruled 1438–81) and his uncle Dom Afonso I, Duke of Braganza (1377–1461) faced off against the Infante Pedro, Duke of Coimbra (1392–1449). Pedro, who was the son of King João I of Portugal and his wife Philippa of Lancaster, met his death at the battle, possibly in combat or perhaps assassinated by one of his own men. As stated in the *Deeds of the Twelve of England* Pedro was Afonso V's uncle, and he also became his father-in-law when his daughter the Infanta Isabel of Coimbra (1432–55) became Afonso V's first wife on May 6, 1447. Álvaro Vasques de Almada, who by this time was Count of Avranches, is known to have been decapitated in the battle.[6]

---

[5] The best treatment of this battle in English is that of Russell, *The English Intervention in Spain & Portugal in the Time of Edward III & Richard II*, pp. 357–99. In Portuguese, see the richly illustrated account by Monteiro, *Aljubarrota 1385. A Batalha Real*, esp. pp. 62–121. There is now also a superb interactive web site about the battle, in Portuguese and English, created by the Fundação Batalha de Aljubarrota: www.fundacao-aljubarrota.pt.

[6] See Baquero Moreno, *A Batalha de Alfarrobeira*, vol. II, pp. 999–1007.

The precise chronology of the *Deeds of the Twelve of England* is nebulous, but roughly framed by these two battles, from which we can deduce that the story was originally composed after the battle of Alfarrobeira and before the approximate date of composition of the only known manuscript copy, that is, some time between 1449 and 1550. Since the battle of Aljubarrota was still a fresh memory I would conjecture that the *Deeds of the Twelve of England* was most likely composed in the fifteenth century, after which it was copied and transmitted, surviving the vicissitudes of time in this one remaining codex. Artur de Magalhães Basto has argued persuasively that the similarities between this prose version and Camões' poetic rendition in *The Lusíads*, along with the fact that the Porto manuscript was once housed in the archives of the Monastery of Santa Cruz in Coimbra, where Camões was Prior, indicate that a version of the original fifteenth-century prose text—if not this very manuscript—was the poet's source and inspiration for his own rendition of the tale.[7]

From a paleographic standpoint the handwriting of Ms. 87 confirms that the same amanuensis who transcribed this copy of Lopes' chronicle also transcribed the *Deeds of the Twelve of England*. It is logical to assume that he perceived a connection between the two texts and married them in this single volume. It is, however, a curious marriage, as the only tangible connections between the two texts are some characters and settings; stylistically they could not be further apart, which helps to explain why the *Deeds of the Twelve of England* is tucked away discreetly at the end of Lopes' chronicle, almost as an afterthought. Perhaps this text was understood to be a condensed, "fun" version—one that would have lent itself easily to theatrical performance—of the complex and serious chronicle that precedes it.

At the end of the text the author states that: "there is a chronicle in England about these matters, which refers to these knights at length." This remark is, ironically, a part of the fiction. The convention of *auctoritas*, designed to testify

---

7 Magalhães Basto, *O essencial sobre Os Doze de Inglaterra*, pp. 7–11. On Camões' reliance on medieval source material see also Santos, "O Medievalismo en Camões. Os Doze de Inglaterra."

to the veracity of the narrative, is a commonplace that ties the *Deeds of the Twelve of England* rhetorically to the Arthurian romance tradition. To cite but one example, *Perceval: The Story of the Grail*, by Chrétien de Troyes, also hinges on the conceit that the author is putting into rhyme a tale that is set down authoritatively somewhere else, in this case a book given to him by Philip of Alsace.[8] This and other Arthurian romances were widely circulated in medieval Portugal, both in the original French, and in Portuguese and Galician-Portuguese translation.[9] The hyperbole that saturates the twelve folios that constitute the *Deeds of the Twelve of England* only adds to the Arthurian flavor, making the work a somewhat frivolous appendage, a chivalric folly juxtaposed with an otherwise remarkably accurate and well-researched chronicle about the reign of King João I.

The Cast of Characters

Who were the Twelve of England? The candid answer is that we do not know, or at least we do not know the names of all twelve. It can be inferred from the text that the twelve Portuguese knights performed great feats of arms at the battle of Aljubarrota, thereby ensuring their ironclad reputation as consummate chivalric warriors. Two names are provided in full in the earliest version, along with another two partial names. They are: Álvaro Gonçalves Coutinho, Álvaro de Almada, Pacheco, and Pedro Homem. These are historical personages who have been inserted into what is at its core a fiction.

The earliest published versions of the tale of the Portuguese knights who travel to England suggest two distinct versions or branches of the tale. Prior to Camões, for example, Jorge Ferreira de Vasconcellos published his *Memorial das proezas da Segunda Tavola Redonda* (*Summary of the Deeds of the Second Round Table*, 1567), in which there is a tantalizingly cryptic reference not to twelve, but

---

[8] Chrétien de Troyes, *Arthurian Romances*, trans. Owen, pp. 374–5. On this particular rhetorical convention see also Stevens, *Medieval Romance*, pp. 211–15.

[9] See Hutchinson, "Anglo-Portuguese Relations and Arthurian Revival in Portugal"; and the overview by Miller, "Hispanic Arthurian Literature." In Portuguese, see Vargas Díaz-Toledo, "A literatura cavaleiresca portuguesa: estado da questão."

thirteen Portuguese knights performing a deed of arms in England on behalf of thirteen damsels.[10] This is a variant of the same story, but no names or further details are provided. To the best of my knowledge it is the only version of the tale that involves thirteen knights. Subsequently, a number of sixteenth- and seventeenth-century works also tell a version of the tale that is clearly derived from the same textual tradition as *The Lusíads* and the manuscript edited in the present volume. The version by Pedro de Mariz in his *Dialogos de varia historia* (*Dialogues on Miscellaneous History*) published in 1598, has an identical dénouement, and the same four knights are named.[11] Similarly Manoel Correa, in his edition of *The Lusíads* with a prose commentary, called *Os Lusíadas do grande Luis de Camõens* (*The Lusíads by the Great Luis de Camões*, 1613), includes the names exactly as they appear in the text edited in the present volume, and a fifth name—João Pereira Agostin—works its way into the tale.[12] By 1624 the chronicler Manuel Soeiro in his *Anales de Flandes* (Annals of Flanders), written in Spanish, claimed to have identified all twelve knights, and dated the deed of arms that they fought in England to the year 1390, though in reality these details are pure speculation on his part. Manuel de Faria e Sousa plagiarized this account in his Spanish commentary on *The Lusíads*, published in 1639.[13] In 1677 the chronicler Fernando de Menezes plagiarized the versions of Ferreira de Vasconcellos and Correa, but listed only the name of Álvaro Gonçalves Coutinho.[14] Subsequently in the eighteenth century two works appeared in print that are loosely based on the version edited here: José Soares da Silva, *Memórias para a Historia de Portugal* (*Studies on the History of Portugal*, 1730–34); and Ignacio Rodrigues Védouro, *Desafio dos doze de Inglaterra* (*The Duel of the Twelve of England*, 1732). These works pad out and expand upon the earlier sixteenth- and seventeenth-century

---

[10] Ferreira de Vasconcellos, *Memorial das proezas da Segunda Tavola Redonda*, p. 324.

[11] Mariz, *Dialogos de varia historia*, p. 140r.

[12] Correa, *Os Lusíadas do grande Luis de Camõens*, p. 175v.

[13] Soeiro, *Anales de Flandes*, vol. II, pp. 26b–27a; and Faria e Sousa, *Lusíadas de Luis de Camões*, vol. II, columns 100–1 (for the date), and 112–13 (alleged identities of the knights).

[14] Menezes, *Vida e Acçõens d'el Rey Dom João I*, pp. 339–44 (reference to Álvaro Gonçalves Coutinho on p. 341).

iterations of the tale, in particular that of Menezes, also listing all of the names of the purported Twelve of England for the reader's satisfaction, even though it bears repeating that the earliest documentary evidence lists only four or five knights, and there is no other solid evidence that proves who the remaining seven or eight were or even *could* have been. Like Soeiro and Faria e Sousa, Rodrigues Védouro postulates a specific date for the deed of arms in England, which according to him took place in 1396.[15]

With the exception of the four knights who are named in whole or in part in the earliest written version of the *Deeds of the Twelve of England*, "The Spurious Eight" (or Seven if we count João Pereira Agostin) are best named in a footnote only.[16] Despite the positivist urge to identify each and every knight by name, I would argue that the seductive allure of this text is that the identities of the twelve Portuguese knights (not to mention their twelve English opponents, the elusive "Duchess," and her twelve ladies-in-waiting) are so shrouded in mystery. I would like to leave the door wide open so that audacious readers, especially those with Portuguese (or even Portuguese-sounding) surnames, who have no noble pedigree to speak of, can insinuate themselves with impunity into this pseudo-history of which they were never a part, and claim to be descendants of the Twelve of England, thereby adding luster to their own heritage, as I believe they were implicitly invited to do when the tale was originally composed in the Middle Ages.

---

[15] Soares da Silva, *Memórias para a Historia de Portugal*, vol. III, pp. 1364–72; Rodrigues Védouro, *Desafio dos doze de Inglaterra*, p. 3 (for the proposed date). These early works are also mentioned by Magalhães Basto and Costa, *Relação ou Crónica breve das cavalarias dos Doze de Inglaterra*, pp. vii–xvi, and Hutchinson, "*Os Doze de Inglaterra*: A Romance of Anglo-Portuguese Relations in the Later Middle Ages?," p. 169.

[16] According to Soeiro and Faria e Sousa the names are as follows: (1) Álvaro Gonçalves Coutinho (Magriço); (2) Álvaro Vasques de Almada; (3) Pedro Homem da Costa; (4) Lope Fernandes Pacheco; (5) Álvaro de Almada (nephew of Álvaro Vasques de Almada, also known as "The Jouster"); (6) João Pereira Agostin; (7) Ruy Gomes da Silva; (8) Álvaro Mendes Cerveira; (9) Ruy Mendes Cerveira; (10) Martin Lopes de Azevedo; (11) Luis Gonçalves Malafaya; and (12) Soeiro da Costa. See Soeiro, *Anales de Flandes*, vol. II, p. 27a, and Faria e Sousa, *Lusíadas de Luis de Camões*, vol. II, columns 112–13. Rodrigues Védouro plagiarizes this list in his *Desafio dos doze de Inglaterra*, p. 5. For further speculation about the identities of the Portuguese knights, see the entry on "The Twelve of England" in the online encyclopedia *Wikipedia*: http://en.wikipedia.org/wiki/The_Twelve_of_England.

The fact that only one manuscript copy of the earliest version of the *Deeds of the Twelve of England* has survived to the twenty-first century should not trick us into believing that it is a rare or obscure text. The text as it is included in the sixteenth- and seventeenth-century printed books just mentioned is so close to Ms. 87 of the Biblioteca Pública Municipal of Porto that these works prove beyond any reasonable doubt that this version, or versions of this version, were at one time widely circulated and easily accessible. The world of medieval manuscripts is a mysterious one, and there could be a thousand possible reasons why just one copy of this text has survived the vicissitudes of time. We should be grateful that one manuscript *has* survived. It would not be too fanciful to suggest that others have as well; they just have not yet been discovered by modern researchers.

The four named knights in the earliest iteration of the *Deeds of the Twelve of England*—Álvaro Gonçalves Coutinho, Álvaro de Almada, Pacheco, and Pedro Homem—and their eight unnamed companions in arms are defined primarily by their regional origin. The reference in the text to the Mountain Range of the Star and their home towns of Trancoso and Pinhel lead Riley to believe that the story is one of regional interest and that it was possibly composed in this region, that is, the Beira province of Portugal.[17] My own view is that the written version that has come down to us is a sophisticated iteration and arrangement of tales of knight-errantry that circulated widely in Europe and are part of a long tradition with a much earlier provenance. The simple act of modifying, adapting or adding specific names for some characters has allowed the author of this version to adapt old tales to new sets of political circumstances for added effect that would have had a more direct and meaningful impact upon a contemporary audience.

The first character mentioned is Álvaro de Almada, who is described as the Count of Avranches. This is a reference to the Portuguese knight of flesh and blood Álvaro Vasques de Almada (died 1449). King Henry VI of England

---

[17] Riley, *Os Doze de Inglaterra: Ficção e Realidade*, pp. 52–3 and 85.

conferred upon him the title Count of Avranches when this region in northern France was English territory, at the same time that Vasques de Almada was, by unanimous acclaim, inducted into the Order of the Garter, on August 4, 1445.[18] The text mentions only the conferral of the noble title, and makes no reference to the English chivalric Order of the Garter.

The second person mentioned is Álvaro Gonçalves Coutinho (1393–1432 or 1433), also known variously as Magriço or The Magriço, meaning "the Lean One," from the Portuguese adjective *magro*—thin, or lean. According to the text, he is from Trancoso or Pinhel, towns that sit at the foot of the wild and vast Mountain Range of the Star, the highest mountain range in Portugal. It is known that the historical Álvaro Gonçalves Coutinho incurred the ire of King João I in the wake of a poorly negotiated marital alliance, after which he went into a self-imposed exile and traveled extensively in Europe, including France and Burgundy. During his historical travels, which took place around 1411–15, he performed feats of arms in France and Burgundy, possibly with the aim of restoring his reputation at the Portuguese royal court.[19] That said, the story as narrated in the *Deeds of the Twelve of England* places the fictional Magriço in Burgundy in the 1430s, by which time it is known that his real-life counterpart was back in Portugal. Also in the context of his story as it unfolds in the manuscript, Coutinho is led to England via France, and thence to Burgundy not because of anything he did, but because of a scandal at the Duke of Lancaster's court instigated by miscreant English knights, and a subsequent request submitted to him by the Duchess of Burgundy.

True to his origins, the fictional Magriço is himself something of a paradox, underscored by the fact that he hails from a liminal space at the crossroads of civilization and barbarism. He is a paragon of Portuguese chivalry, and yet it transpires that he is acutely embarrassed by the fact that he is covered in hair

---

18 See Baquero Moreno, *A Batalha de Alfarrobeira*, vol. II, p. 1004.

19 See Oliveira, *A Casa dos Coutinhos*, pp. 41 and 53–8; and Riley, *Os Doze de Inglaterra: Ficção e Realidade*, pp. 136–8.

and because of his condition he is reluctant to allow the damsel whose honor he saves to wash and kiss his hands in obeisance. Riley suggests that the anonymous author is describing a specific medical condition called localized hypertrichosis, which would explain abnormal hair growth on the fingers and hands.[20] It is doubtful, however, that the anonymous medieval author of this text would have been in any way conversant with such a condition, and more likely in my view that he is tying Magriço typologically to the long-standing biblical tradition of the man whose abundance of hair connotes great strength, a latter-day Samson (though Magriço's lady is no Delilah). His appearance also resonates with popular characters in medieval courtly literature such as the *wodewose*, or wild man (fig. 3, p. 47), and the lycanthropic superhero-knight, among the finest character studies of which are Bisclavret in the twelfth-century *lai* of the same name by Marie de France, and Gorlagon the Werewolf of Arthurian legend.[21] These typological connections lend credence to the argument that the *Deeds of the Twelve of England* has one foot firmly planted in a long and rich narrative tradition that pre-dates the political setting of the tale as it has been set down in the extant manuscript. From a stylistic perspective Magriço's wild appearance dovetails neatly with his origins in the rugged mountainous regions of Portugal and forms a striking contrast with his modest, controlled and courtly demeanor.

The two Portuguese knights who are only partially named are Pedro Homem and Pacheco. It is impossible to say with certainty who these men were. Pedro Homem is possibly the fictional counterpart of a real-life squire to the Infante Dom Pedro, in whose army he fought at the battle of Alfarrobeira in 1449. He was subsequently pardoned for espousing the rebel cause

---

20 Riley, *Os Doze de Inglaterra: Ficção e Realidade*, p. 189.

21 The twelfth-century *lais* of Marie de France are accessible in English. For *Bisclavret*, see *The Lais of Marie de France*, trans. Burgess and Busby, pp. 68–72. Similarly, see *Arthur and Gorlagon the Werewolf*, in *Latin Arthurian Literature*, ed. and trans. Day, pp. 208–35. Medieval Iberian superhero culture is broadly and masterfully analyzed by Harney, "Amadís, Superhero."

by King Afonso V in 1452.[22] Pacheco is possibly the counterpart of João Fernandes Pacheco, the victor of the battle of Trancoso. At this battle in July 1385 a superior Castilian force attacked an inferior Portuguese force, but the Portuguese won due to prudent strategy, taking up a defensive position and awaiting the enemy in highly-disciplined close formation on open ground.[23] The battle of Trancoso was a prelude to, and a rehearsal of, Aljubarrota, the other spectacular Portuguese victory against overwhelming odds that figures so prominently in the narrative. According to the chronicle of the reign of King João I by Fernão Lopes that is coupled with the *Deeds of the Twelve of England* in Ms. 87 of the Biblioteca Pública Municipal of Porto, it was at the battle of Aljubarrota that João Fernandes Pacheco delivered the following harangue to King João I and the Portuguese heavy cavalry, based on his experiences at Trancoso:

> My Lord, you must be very strong and have no fear of their vast numbers, as I know you will not. And I say to all your men: Be not afraid that there are so many of them, as you well can see. If you knew them as I do—for just recently I bathed my hands in their blood—you would understand that there is very little to fear from them. You should dread one thing only, and that is the great travail that you must endure in order to kill so many men, for God deigned to slaughter with His power all those who fell at the siege of Lisbon, and now He commands you to slaughter at will those who survived and have come here to meet their deaths at His hands![24]

---

[22] Baquero Moreno, *A Batalha de Alfarrobeira*, vol. II, p. 1041.

[23] The most comprehensive study of the battle of Trancoso is that of Dias Arnaut, *A Batalha de Trancoso*, esp. pp. 66–72 (on Pacheco). For an account of the battle in English, see Russell, *The English Intervention in Spain & Portugal in the Time of Edward III & Richard II*, pp. 379–80 and 394.

[24] Lopes, *Crónica de D. João I*, vol. II, p. 99 (translation mine).

In light of this eloquent and stirring harangue, it is unfortunate that Pacheco receives just a passing mention and is not given a voice in the *Deeds of the Twelve of England*.

The Portuguese knights are complemented by the presence in the text of other major European historical figures, a common unifying thread being the link forged between the Portuguese house of Avis and the English house of Lancaster in the late fourteenth century. The Duke of Lancaster referred to in the first part of the text is John of Gaunt (1340–99; fig. 4, p. 48). Fernão Lopes' description of him in 1386 when he was 46 years old (though Lopes erroneously states that he was about 60) reads as follows:

> This Dom John, Duke of Lancaster, was a well-built man, tall and upright, carrying less weight than one would expect from the size of his frame. He would be about sixty years old but with fewer white hairs than is normal for one of his age. He spoke well and without haste, being self-controlled and good-humored.[25]

John of Gaunt was initially attracted to matters Iberian through serendipitous acts of marriage, murder, and monarchical mayhem. King Pedro I of Castile had been brutally assassinated in 1369 by his own psychotic half-brother who usurped the throne of Castile and León as King Enrique II that year. Because Gaunt had taken as his second wife King Pedro's daughter, Constanza, he was, after Pedro's murder, now the Pretender *jure uxoris* to the throne of Castile. In the wake of Enrique II's death in 1379 the throne was inherited by Enrique's son King Juan I (1358–90; ruled 1379–90). John of Gaunt subsequently arranged for Catherine of Lancaster, his daughter by Constanza, to marry King Juan's son the future King Enrique III (1378–1406; ruled 1390–1406). The two were wed in 1388, thereby forging yet another link between Castile and England, this time through a deliberately strategic marital alliance in an effort to strengthen John

---

[25] Lopes, *The English in Portugal 1367–87*, ed. and trans. Lomax and Oakley, p. 213.

of Gaunt's own claim to the Castilian throne, a claim that he would ironically renounce entirely at the Treaty of Bayonne that same year, due to the turn of events in the wake of Aljubarrota.

The assassination of King Pedro on March 23, 1369 is graphically portrayed in one of the unique pen and ink drawings in a manuscript copy of Alonso de Cartagena's *Genealogía de los Reyes de Castilla* (Genealogy of the Monarchs of Castile) which dates to ca. 1463 (fig. 5, p. 49). Enrique is shown in the act of stabbing his half-brother through the eye outside the castle of Montiel. To the side are the key stake-holders in what had to have been one of Europe's most dysfunctional families at the time. The figure at the top is "Doña Blanca," that is, Blanche of Bourbon (died 1361), Pedro's wife, whom he married in 1353. Beneath her is Doña María de Padilla (died 1361), Pedro's concubine. Although Pedro was rumored to have secretly married María de Padilla in 1353, it is highly unlikely that he did, and he publicly forsook her so as to make way for Blanche of Bourbon and thereby secure a strategic alliance with France. Never the most astute of diplomats, he then promptly forsook Blanche just three days into the marriage, and returned to the arms of his mistress. Blanche died without issue at the tender age of twenty-five. Although she may well have died of natural causes, a rumor about her premature death persisted at the time that she had been poisoned, and she is duly shown drinking from a poisoned chalice. Pedro's relationship with María de Padilla continued until her own death in the same year as the unfortunate Blanche; in her portrait she is gloating and looking into a mirror, a symbol of vanity. She bore Pedro four children, one of whom, Doña Constanza, is shown next to her husband John of Gaunt, the Duke of Lancaster. Beneath them are their daughter Catherine ("Doña Catalina" in the drawing) and her husband King Enrique III of Castile; both are depicted holding hands and, apparently, living happily ever after.[26]

[26] For concise and eloquent accounts in English of this complex and turbulent period in the history of Castile, see MacKay, *Spain in the Middle Ages*, pp. 119–31, and O'Callaghan, *A History of Medieval Spain*, pp. 419–27.

For all the Duke of Lancaster's personal interest in the throne of Castile, it was also very much in the national interest to secure an alliance between England and Portugal, ostensibly to protect England's as well as Portugal's own incipient seaborne empires from Castilian interference. And even more pressing than the issue of future imperial and maritime expansion was the immediate threat that if the Duke's diplomatic machinations failed, and Castile allied with Portugal as well as France, England would have been vulnerable to invasion and conquest by a formidable triple axis. With these concerns in mind, shortly after the battle of Aljubarrota, the Duke of Lancaster brokered an important alliance between England and Portugal that was ratified at the Treaty of Windsor (1386).

Fig. 6 (p. 50) depicts the Duke of Lancaster and King João I of Portugal seated at the banqueting table at their first historic meeting in person at Ponte do Mouro on November 2, 1386. At this meeting King João I fully exploited to his own advantage John of Gaunt's failure that year to successfully prosecute his claim to the throne of Castile in the wake of the disastrous English invasion of that country. It was at Ponte do Mouro that both parties finalized the accord that King João would now ally with the Duke of Lancaster in the invasion of León and Castile and that he would cement that alliance, ratified at the Treaty of Windsor, by consenting to marry Philippa of Lancaster (1359–1415), the Duke's daughter by his first wife.[27] From King João's point of view the victory at Aljubarrota and the ensuing treaty with England all but extinguished the threat of invasion from Castile by land or sea, thereby inaugurating a new era of vast Portuguese overseas conquests and imperial expansion and, even more importantly, safeguarding Portugal's own independence.

The ensuing Anglo-Portuguese invasion of León in 1387 was a lackluster affair at best: supplies and equipment were inadequate or unsuited to long-range incursions and protracted sieges; the army was plagued by illness exacerbated by the intolerable heat; and much to the surprise and disappointment of King

[27] On the meeting at Ponte do Mouro see Russell, *The English Intervention in Spain & Portugal in the Time of Edward III & Richard II*, pp. 439–42. For readers familiar with Portuguese see also the compelling biography of King João I by Coelho, *D. João I*, pp. 153–7 and 195–8.

João I of Portugal, and the surprise and joy of King Juan I of Castile, the leadership skills of Gaunt himself were called into question. It also became apparent that too few Leonese and Castilians were sympathetic to the Pretender's cause, a weakness that Juan I of Castile exploited to the full; and without collusion simple mathematics dictated that the invading force was not big enough to occupy and maintain long-term control over vanquished territories. After a tense exchange between the King of Portugal and the Duke of Lancaster deep in hostile territory (never a good idea) the campaign was abandoned, ostensibly at King João's insistence.[28] The Anglo-Portuguese alliance got off to a rocky start, with both parties looking out for their own strategic or personal interests. Indeed, as Peter Russell cogently argues, prior to the 1388 Treaty of Bayonne it seems that the Duke of Lancaster would have sacrificed Portugal without any qualms had that been the price to pay in order to secure the throne of Castile, which was always where his most serious pretensions had been.[29]

On a happier note, King João and Philippa took their marital vows in the Cathedral of Porto on February 2, 1387, and their married life began officially on February 14 of that year. Fig. 7 (p. 51) shows the recumbent funerary effigies in the Batalha Monastery of the Portuguese king and his wife Philippa, who even in death are portrayed holding hands, a symbol not only of the strong personal bond that developed between them, but also—despite the shaky start—of the enduring political bond that developed between England and Portugal. It is this marital alliance that is recalled with fondness in the first paragraph of the *Deeds of the Twelve of England.*

As we shall see below, Isabel (1397–1472; fig. 8, p. 52), the daughter of King João I and Philippa of Lancaster, competes closely with Magriço for stealing the show in the third part of the narrative. Isabel became the third wife of Philip the Good, also known as Philip III, Duke of Burgundy (1396–1467; duke 1419–67;

---

28 On the tension between the two at this time see Goodman, *John of Gaunt*, pp. 124–5.

29 Russell, *The English Intervention in Spain & Portugal in the Time of Edward III & Richard II*, pp. 526–48, esp. p. 541. See also Palmer and Powell, *The Treaty of Bayonne (1388) with preliminary Treaties of Trancoso (1387)*, pp. vii–xix.

fig. 9, p. 52) in Bruges on January 7, 1430. It is Philip the Good's cousin King Charles VII of France (1403–61; ruled 1422–61) who provides the antagonistic French connection in the text.

With much chronological and artistic license, it is in the general context of the international diplomacy and intrigue that characterized the relationships between England, France, Burgundy, Castile and Portugal in the late fourteenth and early fifteenth centuries that the narrative unfolds.

Deeds of Arms

The tale of the Twelve of England revolves around a series of deeds of arms, called *cavallarias* in medieval Portuguese. The noun for "knight" in modern Portuguese is *cavaleiro* (with variant spellings in medieval Portuguese); hence the medieval terminology *cavallarias* underscores the fact that deeds of arms were the exclusive domain of members of the knightly caste. However, the details of these combats as they are described in the text are often cryptic and circumstantial. My aim here is to analyze each one to the extent that the record allows.

The Combat of Twelve Against Twelve

As stated by Steven Muhlberger, the formula "X vs. X" for group combats in the Middle Ages was a commonplace, the most famous real-life combat of this type being that of the Thirty against Thirty. This well-documented deed of arms took place on March 16, 1351, and involved two groups of French and English knights.[30] As well as being characterized by violence, Muhlberger argues that all deeds of arms were characterized by what he calls "the centrality of matching words and deeds."[31] The combat of Twelve against Twelve conforms to this typology. As a prelude to, and a pretext for, engaging in physical combat the English knights who instigate the combat of Twelve against Twelve engage in

[30] Muhlberger, *Deeds of Arms*, pp. 72 and 77–111.

[31] *Ibid.*, p. 74.

flyting, a sort of verbal joust that involves hurling insults at one's opponent, often about how ugly or stupid he or she is, with the expectation that the opponent will respond with even more elaborate insults. Jocular, innocuous, and festive, flyting implies that both parties are on an equal footing.

In this instance, however, the festive verbal dueling has a sinister edge, for these men use the language of play to oppress and sexually harass. The English knights focus their attention on the ladies-in-waiting of "the Duchess." According to the text: "One day, while the Duchess' ladies were taking their ease, some English noblemen came and told them that they were very ugly and of too low a class to be the ladies of such an excellent woman as the Duchess." The Duchess could be John of Gaunt's second wife Constanza of Castile (died 1394), who would have been attended by Castilian ladies-in-waiting. Alternatively, she could be his third wife Katherine Swynford (died 1403), who had perhaps inherited some of his previous wife's Castilian ladies-in-waiting, being as they were, permanent fixtures in the ducal household after Constanza's death, which would in turn provide a plausible explanation or motive for the episode as it is described in the text, that is, that these Castilian ladies-in-waiting are not good enough to serve the new English wife. In any event, the ladies-in-waiting are taunted verbally by the men, but because they are not on an equal footing, the ladies react by seeking revenge through a male conduit: they take their complaint not to the Duchess, but directly to the Duke. In doing so they become catalysts, since their complaint to the Duke precipitates a physical fight between two groups that are on an equal footing: the Twelve against Twelve.

It is significant that the Duke turns first to England and then to Portugal for redress. He does not seek assistance from Castile, even though the insulted ladies could well have been Castilian. Hence the text constitutes a curiously backhanded celebration of the Anglo-Portuguese alliance that was forged in the late fourteenth century. The obvious tensions between the English and the Portuguese that permeate the narrative underscores once again the fact that the alliance was, in the late fourteenth century at least, still a very fragile one.

In the text it is the English who set the tension in motion and who first make mention of fighting in the enclosure, in Portuguese *o campo*, which literally means “the field,” the technical legal term to describe the enclosure in which judicial combats were fought. The ladies-in-waiting file an official legal suit or charge against the knights, called a *querella*, that requires the Duke to arrange a formal judicial combat for resolution and closure. The entire process is referred to as the ladies’ *emprise*. As noted by Muhlberger: “The word emprise literally means ‘enterprise, undertaking,’ but … it has the connotation of ‘challenge.’ Emprise also referred to a specific set of commitments and rules.”[32]

Prior to the combat each lady gives her respective Portuguese knight a jewel. This gesture can be interpreted as the bestowal of a love token. Throughout the Middle Ages and Renaissance, however, jewels, in particular diamonds and rubies, were also often distributed as prizes at ducal tournaments.[33] In this case it is significant that the ladies-in-waiting distribute these items before the combat has begun, in symbolic anticipation of victory, in which case the jewel is at once a token and a prize. The English knights are not described as receiving any tokens, and they apparently do not have the support of any ladies as do the Portuguese knights. According to the text, the Portuguese knights enter the enclosure armed at all points in white armor, which refers to plate armor of polished steel with no decoration. The overall effect of a plain harness worn with a glistening jewel, such as a ruby, around the neck would have been quite striking.

With the exception of the armor worn by the Portuguese knights,[34] the weaponry—“iron maces”—and the fact that the deed of arms takes place in an enclosure and lasts a long time, further details about the technicalities and

---

32 Muhlberger, *Jousts and Tournaments*, p. 22.

33 See Neste, *Tournois, joutes, pas d’armes dans les villes de Flandre à la fin du Moyen Âge (1300–1486)*, p. 92; and Fallows, *Jousting in Medieval and Renaissance Iberia*, pp. 38–40.

34 Medieval Portuguese armor is a largely unexplored field of research. For an enlightening and richly illustrated introduction to the topic see LaRocca, “Afonso ‘the African’ and his Army: The Pastrana Tapestries as a Visual Encyclopedia for the Study of Arms and Armor.”

choreography of the combat are not provided. The maces may have looked similar to the one illustrated in fig. 10 (p. 53).[35] This example is South German and dates to around 1470. The head has six flanges. Like most medieval maces it is relatively small, but although the mere sight of it may not inspire fear, in the right hands this mace would have inflicted much damage and pain. As noted by Kelly DeVries and Robert Douglas Smith, the mace was analogous to the scepter, a symbol of the knight's rulership or feudal nobility.[36] To a medieval audience this weapon would have marked the Portuguese knights as veritable princes among men. The text reads as follows:

> And with these words they commenced their battle with their iron maces, in which they engaged with such great ferocity and fury that, having begun in the morning, they continued for so long that during the hours of Tierce, to everyone's relief, they rested.
>
> And, after they had finished taking a rest for a while, they returned to their battle, where the Portuguese attacked their enemies with such ferocity and vigor that finally eight of them were in very bad shape; and after throwing all of the Englishmen out of the enclosure the Portuguese were the victors.

The combat will have begun early, and possibly ended late. A break was declared from nine o'clock until midday, the three hours that correspond to the hours of Tierce. The fight is described as a particularly fierce one, but the Portuguese stop short of killing their opponents, opting instead to batter and humiliate them by ejecting the English knights ignominiously from the enclosure. As a postscript the Portuguese knights, with an air of truculence and not

---

[35] Capwell, *The Wallace Collection. The Complete Digital Catalogue of European Arms and Armour*, A978; Mann, *Wallace Collection Catalogues. European Arms and Armour: Text with Historical Notes and Illustrations*, vol. II, p. 458; and Norman, *Wallace Collection Catalogues. European Arms and Armour: Supplement*, p. 194.

[36] DeVries and Smith, *Medieval Military Technology*, p. 32.

a little mischief, casually address the judges, telling them that their emprise has been completed and if the judges need anything else to let them know. It can be inferred that this deed of arms was a foot combat, though in his rendition of the tale Camões, perhaps to heighten the drama, takes the liberty of turning it into a mounted tournament mêlée with lances, a wood engraving of which accompanies Faria e Sousa's 1639 commentary on this section of *The Lusíads* (fig. 11, p. 53).[37]

Immediately following this deed of arms we are taken to the festive world as it should be; one with no sinister undercurrent. The Portuguese knights "went to rest at a palace that had been arranged for this purpose," where a delightful banquet is held in their honor. During the banquet there is an amusing romantic interlude in which Magriço emerges as the wittiest of the twelve Portuguese knights. Upon acquiescing to his anonymous damsel's request that she be allowed to wash and kiss his hands Magriço makes a play on the Portuguese proverb, "Quem pode manda, obedece quem deve" ("She who can, commands; he who must, obeys"), when he says: "But, since the saying goes that she who can, commands, I, as your subject and vassal, am compelled to obey!" Lest we forget, real knights do not flyte to oppress; they flatter and flirt to impress.

Álvaro Vasques de Almada versus The German

The second part of the narrative concerns a solemn judicial combat between Álvaro Vasques de Almada and an unnamed German knight, the reason or pretext for which is an unspecified accusation of treason. As Muhlberger observes: "treason, homicide and other violent crimes that were punishable by death were allowable reasons for a challenge, and only when the crime was secret and not capable of being proved in some other way."[38]

The judge of this deed of arms is described as "the Emperor," an allusion to Sigismund (1368–1437), King of Germany from 1411, and Holy Roman Emperor from 1433 until his death in 1437; hence the chronological parameters can be set

---

37 Faria e Sousa, *Lusíadas de Luis de Camões*, vol. II, between columns 135 and 136. Faria e Sousa's commentary and the accompanying image are tied to stanza 64 of *The Lusíads*.

38 Muhlberger, *Deeds of Arms*, p. 51.

between 1433 and 1437. Riley argues persuasively that this duel is a re-telling of a real judicial combat that took place in Basel in February 1436 between the Portuguese knight Juan de Merlo and a knight by the name of Enrique de Remestán, thereby pinpointing an even more specific date.[39] The thrust behind this duel as it unfolds in the text is not so much to emphasize historical accuracy, but to underscore the valor and integrity of the flower of Portuguese chivalry, and the perfidy and cowardice that underpins the behavior of the knight who represents Germany.

The duel with the German includes some problematic technical terms. The combatants are initially described as fighting with poleaxes, the medieval Portuguese term for which is *bastão*. Figs 12–13 (p. 54) show two views of a poleaxe dating from ca. 1430.[40] This poleaxe has a coronal and a blade that has no edge and seems never to have had one. It also has little in the way of a distal taper, and the top spike is blunt. It is therefore a purposefully rebated weapon of peace to be used in non-lethal tournament combat on foot in the enclosure, rather than a battlefield weapon. That said, this would still have been a dangerous, destructive weapon, and the concussive power of the axe combined with the lethality of its points may have had much more significance than its edge. In the interests of fairness, absolute equality was essential in judicial combats. According to the text the knights are expected to fight "kind for kind," which means that even after deciding upon the weaponry, the weapons of each combatant would be measured and weighed in order to ensure that neither one had an unfair advantage over the other. They would therefore be fighting with comparable weapons in the name of safety and fairness.

Álvaro Vasques de Almada, however, is subsequently described as wielding a guisarme, rendered in medieval Portuguese as *bisarma*. As defined by John Waldman: "The guisarme blade itself is usually a long and quite large,

---

[39] Riley, *Os Doze de Inglaterra: Ficção e Realidade*, pp. 230–3.

[40] Capwell, *The Wallace Collection. The Complete Digital Catalogue of European Arms and Armour*, A925; Mann, *Wallace Collection Catalogues. European Arms and Armour: Text with Historical Notes and Illustrations*, vol. II, p. 441; and Norman, *Wallace Collection Catalogues. European Arms and Armour: Supplement*, p. 189.

new-moon-shaped crescent. … The weapon is not for thrusting, but some forms have a slight indent towards the upper portion of the blade, which would allow a thrusting motion."[41] Despite this terminology in the Portuguese text, chivalric foot combat was invariably fought with poleaxes, as the guisarme was a peasant weapon that would have been inappropriate in this context. The anonymous author's error is forgivable, for the complex taxonomic mysteries of hafted weaponry have only recently been unlocked and were often misunderstood by medieval authors. Although the evidence is circumstantial, it appears that both parties had agreed to fight with poleaxes equipped with hammer heads or straight back spikes like that illustrated in figs. 12–13 (p. 54), but the dastardly German knight suddenly switched his poleaxe for one with what the text calls a "steel hook" in an effort to secure an advantage over his opponent. The hook refers to a *bec-de-faucon*, that is, a poleaxe with a curved beak or fluke, with a hammer head on the other side, rather than an axe blade and rebated coronal. The hammer would have had a jagged, diamond-faceted head like a modern steak-tenderizer, and this type of poleaxe would also have had a dangerous needle-like top spike, like the one illustrated in fig. 14 (p. 54).[42] This example is possibly French, and dates to around 1450. Such weapons were commonly used in foot combats, and if the beak was sharp, rather than rebated, it would have been difficult to tell the difference from a short distance. This is a plausible explanation for this underhanded exchange of poleaxes. It would have been hard to tell what the German was up to until he started tearing off the unfortunate hero's armor and flesh.

In the end Álvaro Vasques de Almada wrestles his opponent to the ground in a headlock, though it is not clear if he kills him, fractures his spine, or renders him unconscious. The takedown by headlock is a recurring conclusion to poleaxe bouts. It was a tactic used by the fifteenth-century Walloon knight

---

41 Waldman, *Hafted Weapons in Medieval and Renaissance Europe*, pp. 165–6.

42 Capwell, *The Wallace Collection. The Complete Digital Catalogue of European Arms and Armour*, A975; and Mann, *Wallace Collection Catalogues. European Arms and Armour: Text with Historical Notes and Illustrations*, vol. II, pp. 456–7.

Jacques de Lalaing in his poleaxe duel against the Welsh squire Thomas Keith, for example, and it is taught by the early-fifteenth-century master at arms Fiore dei Liberi da Premariacco in his illustrated martial arts manual, *Il Fior di Battaglia* (The Flower of Battle, 1409; fig. 15, p. 55).[43] In the context of Vasques de Almada's duel, this particular stratagem serves to underscore the fact that, as if to mock the cheating German, the Portuguese knight wins this judicial combat not with his axe but with his bare hands.

Countess Isabel versus The King of France: A Feminist Deed of Arms?

I must digress for a moment to mention what is tantamount to a feminist deed of arms that involves a cameo appearance by Countess Isabel of Flanders, the beloved daughter of King João I of Portugal and Philippa of Lancaster, and third wife of Philip the Good, Duke of Burgundy. A note of clarification is necessary, in that the Duke of Burgundy is referred to variously in the text as Duke Dom Philip, and the Count of Flanders. He held many titles: Duke of Burgundy, Brabant, Limburg and Luxembourg; Count of Flanders, Artois, Franche Compte, Hainault, Holland, Zeeland, Namur, and Charolais; Marquess of the Holy Roman Empire; and Lord of Friesland.[44] The text refers to Isabel either as the Duchess, Madame Isabel, or the Countess of Flanders.

The historical Isabel was an intellectually gifted, politically astute, articulate, and highly complex individual. In the wake of the Conference of Arras, which Isabel attended with her husband in 1435, she acquitted herself well as the

---

[43] The most detailed account of Lalaing's duel with Thomas Keith is that of Olivier de la Marche, *Mémoires d'Olivier de la Marche*, ed. Beaune and D'Arbaumont, vol. II, pp. 123–9. On Fiore dei Liberi and wrestling techniques see Mondschein, *The Knightly Art of Battle*, pp. 22–9. On the complexities of medieval poleaxe combat and wrestling techniques, see Anglo, "*Le Jeu de la Hache*: A 15th-Century Treatise on the Technique of Chivalric Axe Combat," and Anglo, *The Martial Arts of Renaissance Europe*, pp. 172–201; also Nadot, *Le Spectacle des joutes*, pp. 56–8 and 75–86. In the context of medieval Portugal, wrestling techniques are also discussed by King Duarte I in his *Livro da ensinança de bem cavalgar toda sela* (1434), now available in English translation. See Duarte, *The Art of Riding on Every Saddle*, trans. Preto and Preto, pp. 188–99. A new English translation of this work by Dr. Jeffrey Forgeng is nearing completion.

[44] On Philip's many titles and possessions see Taylor, *Isabel of Burgundy*, pp. 34–7.

Duke's plenipotentiary on two further diplomatic missions to France in 1441 and 1445, both of which were fraught with tension and intrigue as England, Burgundy, and France negotiated and jockeyed for as much power and control as they could each secure in European domains.[45] It is in this historical context that her story unfolds.

In keeping with the pro-Portuguese sentiments that underpin the *Deeds of the Twelve of England*, the fictional Isabel is represented as a strong-willed, fiercely independent personality in contrast to her timid Burgundian husband. In this section of the narrative, Isabel discovers that she has become, through marriage to a Burgundian, subject to certain laws of vassalage imposed upon her husband's family by the centralized French monarchy, a subjugation to which she strenuously objects. Neither her husband nor all the Flemish knights in his court, who cite vague legal reasons for not coming to her defense, will join forces with Isabel in her quest to release Burgundy from French subjugation. The fictional Isabel is metamorphosed, as the product of a high-powered Anglo-Portuguese marriage, into an empowered super heroine, or more appropriately, in the context of stock medieval character types, a "super shrew." Much to her credit, she will neither be tamed nor ignored, either in or by the male-dominated world in which she is compelled to operate. In Isabel's case the anonymous author ingeniously molds a stock character type which typically has negative connotations into a portrayal that encapsulates the best qualities of the Anglo-Portuguese marital alliance. From a political standpoint, in what must have been meant as a double propagandistic slap in the face, it is the Portuguese shrewish wife in her role as plenipotentiary, rather than the Burgundian henpecked husband in his role as premier peer, who proactively defends Burgundy's autonomy in the face of French political oppression.

Women of the noble elite were generally restricted to the household, but Isabel moves far beyond the space associated with her (and her effete husband's)

---

45 For an engaging account in English of these diplomatic missions see Taylor, *Isabel of Burgundy*, pp. 72–101. See also the well-documented book by Sommé, *Isabelle de Portugal, duchesse de Bourgogne*, pp. 402–8.

subjugation, not only traveling to the French king's court, but also taking a throne with her. In her hands a traditional symbol of domesticity, the chair in which the head of the household's wife would be expected to sit submissively, is transformed into a powerful political symbol that the wily Countess uses as a means of challenging the king's authority and even his right to his own throne. Not only that; after menacingly wielding her throne, the redoubtable Isabel engages in the male-dominated, fine art of flyting, and rhetorically emasculates the French king in a verbal duel, just as Magriço will subsequently crush the king's champion in a physical duel.

In the portrait of the Countess of Flanders in fig. 8 (p. 52), the anonymous artist has brilliantly captured her subtly wry smile, which conveys to the viewer that nobody messes with Madame Isabel. Her character would most assuredly have appealed to the female audience of the *Deeds of the Twelve of England*.

Álvaro Gonçalves Coutinho versus The Frenchman

Countess Isabel almost upstages the principal male character in the third section of the narrative, which focuses on a deed of arms between Álvaro Gonçalves Coutinho and an anonymous French knight. Playing once again with stock character types, the anonymous author metamorphoses the French knight, who might be expected to embody the civilized chivalric ideal, into a stock medieval villain, a prideful braggart knight whose comeuppance is inevitable and, from the reader's point of view, enthusiastically anticipated. The type of behavior that he exhibits is condemned in a variety of chivalric codes of conduct. For example, *Las Siete Partidas* (The Seven Divisions), an extensive law code compiled between the years 1256 and 1265 during the reign of King Alfonso X, known as "the Wise," of Castile (1221–84; ruled 1252–84), specifies that pride in the form of bragging and haughtiness is unacceptable except in real battle, and even then it is only permissible for a noble commander to sprinkle a harangue with haughty hyperbole if he thinks it will spur his men to victory. The exact wording is as follows:

> Certain things should be done by knights which, on no account, they should omit, and these are of two kinds, namely: some in word, others in deed. Those which relate to speech are that they should not be low or intemperate in their language, or haughty except under certain circumstances where it is suitable; as, for instance, in martial exploits where they are compelled to reassure their followers and inspire them with a desire to do their duty, calling them by name, entreating them to do the best they can, and censuring them when they know they are guilty of errors, and do not act as they ought.[46]

In a similar vein statute V of the Castilian Order of the Band, a monarchical order of knighthood, the statutes of which are said to have been composed by King Alfonso XI of Castile in 1332, synthesizes the concept as follows: "No Knight of the Band should ever brag about any chivalric deed that he has performed."[47]

As a braggart knight, the French king's champion precedes the joust with a flyting match of the type that characterizes the duels in this particular text, though in this instance both contestants are on an equal footing, and Magriço gives as good as he gets. At this point the French knight is an exaggerated comic figure, not unlike an ogre or giant who, as it were, smells the blood of a Portuguese man. He is, however, about to do battle with a man whose hair and mountainous origins also tie him to the tradition of the mythical giants. This, then, is an equal match.

The verbal duel is followed by a joust and a combat with swords. It is the flocculent flower of Portuguese chivalry who flourishes once again and wins this combat, his laconic demeanor forming a neat antithesis to the Frenchman's

---

[46] Alfonso X, *Las Siete Partidas*, trans. Scott and Burns, II.xxi.22 (vol. II, pp. 429–30).

[47] Ceballos-Escalera y Gila, *La Orden y Divisa de la Banda Real de Castilla*, p. 61 (translation mine).

gross verbosity. Álvaro Gonçalves Coutinho receives his armor and horse from an anonymous count who has made a formal pact of friendship (*amizade*, in the Portuguese original) with the Duke of Burgundy, and is therefore duty-bound by law to afford assistance to the Portuguese knight. Coutinho reminds the count of his duty to both the Order of Chivalry and his formal bond of friendship with the Duke of Burgundy as soon as he meets him. According to the laws of friendship as they are codified in *Las Siete Partidas*: "a man should exert himself for the good of his friends, just as he would for his own advantage."[48] This is exactly what the obliging count does, testing the armor and horse himself in order to ensure victory in the field, before he hands them over to Álvaro Gonçalves Coutinho.

The deed of arms begins with a joust of war. The thrusts delivered by the two knights with their lances unhorse both opponents, who then continue to fight on foot with swords. Figs. 16–17 (pp. 56–57) are illustrations from a sixteenth-century English manuscript currently housed in the College of Arms in London, Ms. M.6. The armor depicted in these illustrations is from a later period than that of the *Deeds of the Twelve of England*, but the principal types of lance-strokes are the same as those that would have been delivered by Álvaro Gonçalves Coutinho and his French opponent. They are as follows: striking the head; striking coronal to coronal;[49] striking the chest; and making an attaint—a light or average hit which is perfectly respectable but does not break the lance—versus a full hit that splinters the lance, with the caption, "Note that the Lorde Darcy was not overthrown, but to shew the maner of the breking of the speares." Thrusts to the head and chest in particular were not uncommon, and could precipitate falls from horses. The coronal, however, was a type of lance-head used for jousts of peace, with special tines that would either lock onto the opponent's armor or shield without piercing through, or possibly onto

48 Alfonso X, *Las Siete Partidas*, trans. Scott and Burns, IV.xxvii.5 (vol. IV, p. 1005).

49 Drawings of the lance-strokes to the head and coronal to coronal that are clearly derived from those in College of Arms, Ms. M.6 can also be found in London, British Library, Ms. Harley 69, *The Booke of Certaine Triumphes*, fols. 19v and 20r.

his coronal. This safety lance-head was vastly different from the type of sharp point that would have been used in the joust of war between Magriço and the Frenchman (see figs. 18 and 19 [p. 58], respectively). The illustrations in College of Arms Ms. M.6 represent the most ideal scoring opportunities, for in reality striking coronal to coronal was extremely rare, virtually impossible to do by design, and a difficult stroke to judge. The following is an eye-witness account from a sixteenth-century Spanish joust that underscores the rarity of the stroke and the confusion it could cause among the judges:

> I saw that in one course the tips of the lances locked rochet against rochet, and Don Pero Vélez's lance broke and with that he equalised or had broken as many lances as Gutierre Quixada. But Gutierre Quixada averred that although Don Pero Vélez's lance had broken, Gutierre Quixada rather than Don Pero Vélez broke it, for because his lance was stronger it remained intact and he had broken the other man's lance, and that that lance should not be counted as a lance broken for Don Pero Vélez but as a lost and weak lance, and it should be counted as a lance broken to Gutierre Quixada. The judges of this joust were the Duke of Alba Don Fadrique de Toledo, and Lord Antonio de Fonseca, who were to judge all the jousters including these two knights since they were two of the jousters. But the private and loyal judges working on behalf of Gutierre Quixada and Don Pero Vélez were other men, and they either could not or would not settle the dispute, and they accepted as arbitrator the opinion of the King. And it turned out to be such a subtle point that no resolution could be reached at that time, because the King insisted on giving careful consideration, but there was no lack of opinions about it and there is much to say for and against.[50]

---

[50] Cited in Fallows, *Jousting in Medieval and Renaissance Iberia*, p. 217.

In a joust of war, striking point to point by design would have been beyond the capability of even the most skilled jouster; the target was simply too small to locate and hit with accuracy. The strokes that unhorsed both opponents in the joust described in the *Deeds of the Twelve of England* were therefore most likely to the head or chest.

Carlos Guilherme Riley and Ana Maria Rodrigues have shown that, like the duel with the German, this joust is loosely based on some real jousts that took place in Paris from October 11, 1414 through February 23, 1415 during the latter stages of the Hundred Years' War, and that are well-documented in contemporary chronicles.[51] In the *Deeds of the Twelve of England* the chronology of these jousts and Countess Isabel's diplomatic missions to France between 1435 and 1445 is inverted and telescoped into one episode that acquires a new dimension in keeping with medieval romance fiction:[52] that of the imprisoned lady who is freed from captivity, thanks to the intervention and the martial skills of a peerless knight-errant. The fact that Isabel must rely on a Portuguese knight for succor, as opposed to her own husband or any other Flemish knight, undoubtedly furthers the Portuguese cause. Within this framework the anonymous author takes the liberty of molding Álvaro Gonçalves Coutinho into the Portuguese champion of the Portuguese-born Countess Isabel.

Magriço and his opponent are described as fighting in an enclosure, which is designed to corral them. At the end of the combat the author for once is not elliptic, and there is no question that Álvaro Gonçalves Coutinho cuts off his opponent's head. Climactic decapitation is the definitive way of vanquishing and silencing a verbose opponent. The episode in the *Deeds of the Twelve of England* is not dissimilar to one described succinctly in a contemporary Castilian ballad, as follows:

---

51 Riley and Rodrigues, "Les Joutes d'Alvaro Gonçalves Coutinho à Paris."

52 On the collapsed time-line of these events, see also Hutchinson, "*Os Doze de Inglaterra*: A Romance of Anglo-Portuguese Relations in the Later Middle Ages?," p. 173.

Neath a green pine,
they fight each other with lances,
now they have come to the axes;
the prideful one falters,
and after falling flat on the ground,
he cut off his head
without having any advantage.[53]

This motif translated smoothly to the world of manuscript illumination. Fig. 20 (p. 59) is a dramatic rendition of a similar scene from a fifteenth-century illuminated manuscript that depicts the conclusion of the real-life deed of arms fought before the King of France between Jean de Carrouges and Jacques Le Gris on November 27, 1386.[54] In this illumination Carrouges has left the enclosure, and, with his long dagger leaning on his shoulder, is calmly walking towards the embrace of his wife Marguerite. A squire is inside the enclosure, gingerly holding the freshly severed head of Jacques Le Gris as the King looks on. Eye-witness accounts of this deed of arms, however, concur that Le Gris was killed by a stab wound through the throat that was certainly vicious, but did not sever the victim's head from his body. The fifteenth-century illuminator of this fourteenth-century deed of arms has thus added a spurious detail in his own dramatization of the event, in consonance with the ever popular decapitation motif. We are once again at the kaleidoscopic intersection of reality and romance, where knights prove their mettle, virility, and martial skill in deeds of arms by slicing off their opponents' heads, and the decapitation itself becomes a motif in the literary and pictorial representation of deeds of arms both real and imagined.

---

53 *Spanish Ballads*, ed. Smith, no. 57, lines 26–32, p. 113 (translation mine). On the beheading motif in medieval chivalric romance see Ward, "To Be a 'Fleschhewere': Beheading, Butcher-Knights, and Blood Taboos in *Octavian Imperator*"; also Guerreau-Jalabert, *Index des Motifs Narratifs*, p. 171, motif Q 421.

54 This deed of arms is the subject of the best-selling book by Jager, *The Last Duel*, esp. pp. 165–85.

Thematically this section of the *Deeds of the Twelve of England* is parallel to the first section in that no Flemish knights step forward to restore the Portuguese Countess' honor, just as no English knights would step forward to restore the honor of the Duchess' ladies-in-waiting. It will once again be up to the flower of Portuguese chivalry to save the day. With linguistic as well as thematic juxtaposition in mind, another subtle link between the first and third sections is the repetition of the verb *aportar* ("to come to port"). In the first section the third-person plural verb form—*aportaram* ("they came to port")—signifies the glorious and public arrival in London of the near-cohesive group of Portuguese champions clad in their resplendent armor. In the third section the third-person singular verb form—*aportou* ("he came to port")—indicates Álvaro Gonçalves Coutinho's solitary and surreptitious arrival in Paris by boat on the river Seine, dressed now in the garb of a humble pilgrim.

Like many of the comic-book superheroes of the twenty-first century who are defined and identified by their iconic outfits, so too the Portuguese knights become what and who we expect them to be when they don their armor, the iconic kit of the medieval action hero, as they uphold justice against the English, German and French super villains. The attraction to heroes whose special powers are revealed or unmasked only when they cover themselves up or put on the mask is surely one of the greatest and most enduring chivalric paradoxes. It is not clear from the text if each of the Portuguese knights has his own particular skill-set with different types of weapons. What is clear is that once fully armored they are an unstoppable force; eminently capable, if necessary, of "terminating with extreme prejudice," to borrow a modern military euphemism.

With the exception of Álvaro Vasques de Almada, the Portuguese knights—and the feisty daughter of a king who has Portuguese as well as English blood coursing through her veins—always win. According to the text, when Álvaro Vasques de Almada was asked by panic-stricken Prince Dom Pedro what he planned to do in the face of their impending doom at the battle of Alfarrobeira, he replied: "Sire, have lunch here, and then have dinner in Hell!" His desperate last words and tragic fate demonstrate that a knight-errant can lose his super powers and is not indestructible or invincible if he marshals those powers unwisely. If his ignominious death underscores the futility of civil wars and the penalty for treachery against one's own kith and kin, the moral that can be inferred from the other deeds of arms described in this text is that alliances, however tenuous they may be in the early days, can with care, diplomacy, and martial skill often lead to peace, prosperity, and above all, independence.

Conclusion

This curious yet highly engaging text is in my view an essay on chivalric conduct, based on a synergistic interface between romance, reality, and theatrical performance that also captures the frosty friendship and the tensions that characterized the early, uneasy days of the Anglo-Portuguese alliance. Emerging nationalist sentiments reflect the Portuguese desire to be at the center of the western chivalric world. Like the text itself, which stands at the margin of a much broader codex, the Portuguese heroes in the text are from a country at the periphery of Europe. As quintessential knights-errant they then move to England, to France, to Germany, and finally to Burgundy, which has appropriately been called "a veritable epicenter of knight-errantry."[55]

The Anglo-Portuguese alliance is celebrated in the text with a strictly Portuguese bias in mind. The Twelve are asked to perform deeds of arms in foreign lands, and they do this loyally as a cohesive team, acquitting themselves brilliantly in each locale; they neither waiver nor shift their allegiance as the English knight John of Gaunt did between Castile and Portugal. They are nothing less than the embodiment of loyalty, one of the cardinal chivalric virtues that is emphasized in a broad array of medieval texts. Wolfram von Eschenbach (fl. ca. 1195–1225) notes in *Parzival*, for example: "Chivalry is endowed with two rich revenues: a true sense of shame, and noble loyalty." King Alfonso X of Castile likewise states in *Las Siete Partidas* that knights "should be perfect in loyalty and in truth;" and, he adds: "Loyalty is more precious than lineage, or any other

---

[55] Ruiz, *A King Travels*, p. 241.

attribute which can exist." This notion translated smoothly to the first statute of the Castilian Order of the Band, which declares that the Order is founded upon two principles: "the first in praise of Chivalry; the second of Loyalty." And finally, Joanot Martorell, author of the great Catalan chivalric romance *Tirant lo Blanc* (1490), makes the following observation: "A knight should strive, first, to be truthful, second, to be loyal, third, to be strong, fourth, to be generous, fifth, to love justice."[56] He might well have been describing the Twelve of England.

In particular the Portuguese knights' English and French foes are aggressive in word, but lacking in deed; their German foe is nothing less than a cheat. The Portuguese on the other hand are courteous, modest, and gently witty in word, as well as honorable, resilient, and ferociously talented in deed. They are introduced into the text by John of Gaunt, about whose abilities during the disastrous Anglo-Portuguese invasion of León in 1387 Peter Russell makes the following harsh assessment: "It was characteristic of his generalship always that he was incapable of distinguishing objectives which mattered from those which did not;" and: "History cannot acquit Lancaster of having made failure certain by his deficiency in almost every quality required of a commander in the field." Anthony Goodman, while not as harsh as Russell, provides the following laconic summary: "Gaunt seems to have had few eminent Castilian knights available in his company to give him strategic advice."[57] When in doubt, blame the Castilians.

On the basis of these assessments, it is safe to say that the introduction of the Portuguese knights is intentionally ironic. They are introduced by one of the highest-ranking knights in all of England, a scheming, frustrated Pretender with a reputation for shifting loyalties (expedient and necessary though such strategies may have been in the political reality of the time) and ineptitude in the field,

---

[56] Eschenbach, *Parzival*, trans. Hatto, p. 167; Alfonso X, *Las Siete Partidas*, trans. Scott and Burns, II.ix.6 and II.xviii.15 (vol. II, pp. 315 and 390); Ceballos-Escalera y Gila, *La Orden y Divisa de la Banda Real de Castilla*, p. 57 (translation mine); Martorell, *Tirant lo Blanc*, trans. La Fontaine, p. 461.

[57] Russell, *The English Intervention in Spain & Portugal in the Time of Edward III & Richard II*, pp. 466 and 479, respectively; Goodman, *John of Gaunt*, p. 121.

in a conversation about their probity, constancy, and steadfast allegiance, and the stellar reputation for martial prowess that precedes them. They subsequently live up to, if not exceed, all expectations when we finally meet them in person.

Between them the Portuguese knights outclass the Castilians (Aljubarrota), then the English, the Germans, the Burgundians, and the French. Collectively they defeat the most physically or verbally violent representatives of all the major powers in the European chivalric conglomerate of the time. The text can thus be read as an assertion that in the wake of the victories at Trancoso and Aljubarrota, Portugal is a force to be reckoned with, emerging as a major player in the European martial and chivalric arena.

One final note: Most popular movies these days inspire one or more sequels, so what of "The Return of the Twelve of England"? Well, return they did in a very modern, roundabout way. In 1966 the Portuguese national football team traveled to England, where they reached third place in the FIFA World Cup. The obvious parallels of a pre-arranged medieval deed of arms/modern football match between teams of English and Portuguese knights/football players in an enclosed field inspired the Portuguese press to recall the *Deeds of the Twelve of England*. However, the number of knights did not match the number of players, so they cleverly appropriated the nickname of Álvaro Gonçalves Coutinho, and dubbed the Portuguese national team "Os Magriços" ("The Lean Ones"). This nostalgic sobriquet captured the nation's imagination and brought the legendary Twelve of England back to national and international prominence once more. I mention this not as a trivial detail, but because it demonstrates just how alive and vibrant the Middle Ages still are in the modern era.

2.
A Note on Armor

Taking into account the collapsed chronology for the joust described in the third and final section of the narrative, from the context it is possible to speculate that this deed of arms took place in the first half of the fifteenth century, ca. 1414–45. Two rare, surviving harnesses made around this time allow us to contextualize the type of armor that would have been worn by the knights described in the text. These harnesses are armor S18 at Churbug Castle, located in what is now the extreme north of Italy (fig. 21, p. 60), and the Avant armor in the Kelvingrove Museum in Glasgow (figs. 22–24 pp. 61–63). Both of these harnesses were probably worn by members of the Matsch family in the same region but at different times. They represent the state of the art of armor in two crucial points in the development of Italian armor. The two armors have much in common, but also some differences that are worthy of note.

The surviving pieces of Churburg S18 date to about 1420, and represent the final form of Milanese armor at the end of the age of the transition from mail to plate. In its current configuration this armor weighs 58 lbs., 7 oz. (26.67 kg.). The Avant armor, so called because the word "AVANT" ("Forward") is inscribed repeatedly in *pointillé*, or point-work, on the turned edges on the sides of the breastplate, was made in Milan ca. 1438–40 by the Corio family of armorers.[58] This armor is an extremely rare survivor indeed, as it is the earliest near-complete armor in the world, with certain exceptions that should be noted: the right gauntlet is original to the period but from a different, larger armor made by the rival Missaglia workshop; the left gauntlet is a twentieth-century reproduction; and the right gardbrace and tassets are missing. In its current configuration this armor weighs 57 lbs., 5oz. (26 kg.).

Both of these harnesses are field armors designed principally for combat on the battlefield, though they could also have been worn in jousts of war, the purpose of which was to emulate real combat, with no special pieces of jousting safety equipment. In the case of a joust of peace at this time it would also have been possible to adapt war armors such as these by exchanging the field helmet for a specially made jousting helm. An example of a fifteenth-century Portuguese jousting helm from the royal armory of the House of Avis is illustrated in fig. 25 (p. 64) (the trap-door, or cut-out on the right-hand side, which was used for ventilation, is currently displayed in the open position). On the other hand, figs. 26–28 (pp. 65–67) show three different views of portions of a French armor dating to the first half of the fifteenth century which, unlike Churburg S18 and the Avant armor, was specially designed for the joust of peace only, and not for battle as well.[59] This special jousting kit is distinguished by its helm and capacious lance-rest. On this early example the helm was attached to the breastplate by buckles and leather straps as opposed to the long, stout metal clasp known as a charnel, which is clearly visible on the later Portuguese helm illustrated in fig. 25 (p. 64).

---

[58] The most accessible studies of Churburg S18 in English are those of Trapp et al., *The Armoury of the Castle of Churburg*, vol. I, pp. 35–40, and vol. II, pp. 69–73; and Blair et al., *Historic Armour and Arms in the Castle of Churburg*, pp. 23–4, 70–1, and 76–81. On the Avant armor (Glasgow Museums E.1939.65.e) see Capwell, *The Real Fighting Stuff*, pp. 26–9; Fallows, *Jousting in Medieval and Renaissance Iberia*, pp. 72–3; Joubert, *Catalogue of the Collection of European Arms & Armour Formed at Greenock by R.L. Scott*, ed. Woosnam-Savage and Capwell, pp. 9–11; and Woosnam-Savage, "The 'AVANT' Armour and R.L. Scott." I am grateful to Dr. Tobias Capwell, Curator of Arms and Armor at The Wallace Collection in London, for sharing with me his new and as yet unpublished research on the date of this armor.

[59] On this armor, see Reverseau, "L'Habit de guerre des français en 1446. Le manuscrit anonyme fr. 1997 de la Bibliothèque Nationale," pp. 190–7.

Given the theme of judicial combat that permeates the text, particularly the gruesome end result of the duel between Magriço and his anonymous French opponent, it is clear that the author's intent is to describe a joust of war. Only in very serious deeds of arms or trials by combat would the combat begin with a joust of war, followed by combat with swords, either on horseback (after the lances were broken) or on foot (after unhorsing), until somebody got killed.[60] Fig. 29 (p. 68) is a fluid depiction of a mounted combat with swords in the enclosure, the broken lances on the ground indicating that the two knights have just engaged in a joust, but in this case without unhorsing each other. Decapitating a man who was wearing a jousting helm was a deed that even a lycanthropic superhero knight could not hope to accomplish, and in any case both combatants would have been unable to see had they attempted their foot combat with swords in cumbersome jousting helms; solid evidence that the characters are operating here in the world of warlike judicial combat.

The head defense on Churburg S18 is a distinctive example of an early *armet*. The visor, which was originally secured with removable hinge pins, is missing. The armet features a shallow medial ridge and a hole for a crest at the slightly pointed apex. It has two hinged cheek plates. This armet shows no sign of ever having a reinforcing plate at the brow or a rondel at the back, as is the case on later examples. The lower edge is equipped with vervelles for the attachment of a mail aventail.

The Avant armor is currently displayed with a type of helmet called a *barbute*. While this helmet may have belonged to the original owner of the armor, it would not have been the one he would have normally worn with the full harness. In all likelihood, as Tobias Capwell observes,[61] this harness would originally have been worn in combat with an armet like the one illustrated in fig. 30 (p. 69). Like the Churburg armet, this example features a shallow medial ridge, two hinged cheek plates, and the lower edge is also fitted with vervelles for the suspension

---

[60] For precedents of this type of deed of arms see Muhlberger, *Deeds of Arms*, pp. 55–8.

[61] Capwell, *The Real Fighting Stuff*, p. 28.

of a mail aventail. Unlike the Churburg armet, it has a cusped reinforcing plate at the brow, and a provision for a rondel which has survived intact. Also of note is that it retains the original peaked visor with removable hinge pins.

Both harnesses include a full cuirass with a front and back plate with a fauld suspended from a lower plackart attached to the upper cuirass with straps and buckles. The breastplate on the Churburg S18 harness is comprised of a single, large globose plate. This plate is fitted with staples and a lance-rest as well as a large and deeply curved *lisière d'arrêt*, or stop-rib, designed ostensibly to deflect lance-thrusts to the neck. The edges of the arm openings are rolled outward in shallow rolls, but the neck opening is not rolled and is turned strongly outward forming an integral stop-rib for the neck. The lower plackart of this harness is suspended with three straps and buckles in the front and three more in the rear. The plackart is generally rounded in form but does not fit well with either the upper back plate or breastplate. The plackart also has a vaguely conical fauld comprised of three lames. The lower edge of the lowest lame is rolled outward and there is no evidence of tassets ever being attached. The back plate is made up of three elements: a central back plate; and two attached side extensions. The front and rear elements of the cuirass are joined together with a strap that is on the rear plackart and wraps around the front plackart at the waist in the manner of a belt.

Like the Churburg armor, the breastplate on the Avant armor is comprised of a single, large globose plate. This plate is fitted with staples for a lance-rest which is now missing. There is a vestigial stop-rib secured near the neck opening, and the edges of the neck and arm openings are also rolled outward in shallow rolls. Unlike the Churburg armor, which uses a three strap system in the front and rear, the lower plackart of the Avant armor is suspended from the upper cuirass by a single buckle in the front and another in the rear. The plackart closely conforms to the shape of the cuirass and it has a dependent fauld of four lames. The lower edge of the lowest lame is not rolled and there are straps present that demonstrate the position of the missing tassets. The back plate is made up of three horizontal lames attached to a fourth plate that is shaped to fit the upper back. The front and rear elements of the cuirass are joined together with hinges on the left and buckles on the right.

Vambraces, or arm defenses, in the fifteenth century are generally made up of three elements: defenses for the shoulder; defenses for the arms; and defenses for the hands. The arm defenses of Churburg S18 differ from the Avant armor most noticeably in their lack of shoulder defenses. Whether this is due to design or loss is difficult to say. However, since the armor is set up with a lance-rest for jousting it is highly likely that there was originally a set of pauldrons that are now lost. The arm defenses are essentially of the same form as the arms on the Avant armor, with all of the same elements, though they are symmetrical and have smaller wings, more rounded cops and no removable reinforcing plate for the elbow. The gauntlets are broadly similar as well, though there are no mitten lames to defend the fingers. Instead the metacarpal plate is elongated approximately to the same point as the first lame on the Avant gauntlet and each finger is individually defended with small scale-like lames secured underneath a leather covering. Each finger also has an exposed fingertip plate. The cuffs are not quite as wide as those on the Avant armor at the back of the hand, though they are somewhat wider in line with the palm.

The arms on the Avant armor follow a similar pattern. The shoulders are protected with large *pauldrons* which extend far behind the back to the point where they touch but do not overlap as is the case in some later examples. These pauldrons are asymmetrical and consist of upwardly overlapping lames. The right pauldron is cut away from the underarm to accommodate the couching of a lance. As I mentioned above, the left pauldron originally had a removable *gardbrace*, or reinforcing plate, secured by a post and split pin, but this is now missing, having perhaps been prised off and lost in battle, as Capwell speculates.[62] The arm defenses are essentially symmetrical except for the shapes of the fans on the elbow cops, which are asymmetrical, the right one having a large fan and the left with a smaller fan but covered overall with a removable reinforcing

62 Capwell, *The Real Fighting Stuff*, p. 28.

plate. The elements of the arm defenses are joined together with articulating lames; one above the elbow and two below. The lowest lame is joined to the forearm defense with three sliding rivets which allow some measure of lateral rotation of the forearm. The hands are protected by mitten gauntlets (as stated above, the left gauntlet is a twentieth-century replacement, and the right does not match this armor but is from the correct period). The fingers are covered with two mitten type lames which articulate to the metacarpal plate. The cuff is conical in shape and quite wide in line with the back of the hand and narrow in line with the palm.

Like arm defenses, leg defenses in the fifteenth century are generally made up of three elements: defenses for the upper leg, defenses for the lower leg, and defenses for the feet. The leg defenses for Churburg S18 are noticeably different from the Avant armor. The thigh defense is comprised of two elements: a front plate, and a wraparound guard for the back of the leg. Each is made of a single, solid piece, and they are joined with a pair of hinges which are set on the interior of the plates. The knee defense is attached to the thigh plate by means of a single, wide lame which is set on the interior of the thigh plate. This internal arrangement is characteristic of leg defenses shortly after the turn of the fifteenth century. The knee plate has a pointed profile and its wing is smaller and less elaborate than the knee defense on the Avant armor. Below the knee plate there is a single lame and a demi-greave which is not pierced for an alignment pin. The greaves from Churburg S18 are unfortunately missing. This harness may originally have included *sabatons*, or foot defenses, which are also now missing.

In the case of the Avant armor, the thigh is protected with two main elements, upper and lower, which are separated by a strong triangular rolled edge. The backs of the thigh are protected with wraparound guards made of three vertical plates, each having two facets divided by a vertical crease. Each of these elements is joined to the others with a pair of external hinges. The knee defense is joined to the thigh plate with a single articulation lame which is secured to the exterior of the main thigh plate. The knee plate has a pronounced medial crease and a large, faceted wing that wraps backward well behind the knee. Below the knee there are two lames and a demi-greave. This demi-greave is pierced with a hole through which passes a pin secured to the greave proper to keep them in alignment. The greaves are of traditional closed form. The two elements are secured with a pair of external hinges. The lower edge of the greave is not rolled and it is perforated for a mail covering which was used to protect the feet.

3.
A Note on the Edition and Translation

The version of the *Deeds of the Twelve of England* edited and translated in this volume is that of the sole surviving manuscript in Porto. There are several other editions of this text in Portuguese. The most accessible is that of Magalhães Basto (with an introduction by Joaquim Costa) published in 1935, and re-printed without changes in 1986. Magalhães Basto's edition has no philological value, as he modernized the language of the text. His transcription is also at times unusually careless, though in all fairness to him, without the aid of computers, digitized copies on CD and DVD, or even photocopies, working conditions for transcribing manuscripts in Portugal in the year 1935 would not have been nearly as conducive to precision as they are today. Another edition was prepared by Carlos Guilhermo Lopes Riley in 1988. This is a paleographic edition included in Riley's unpublished doctoral dissertation and is not easily available.[63]

---

[63] Magalhães Basto and Costa, *Relação ou Crónica breve das cavalarias dos Doze de Inglaterra*, pp. 89–103; Magalhães Basto, *O essencial sobre Os Doze de Inglaterra*, pp. 19–46; Riley, *Os Doze de Inglaterra: Ficção e Realidade*, pp. 29–36.

For my own edition of the text I have followed the sole surviving manuscript copy, Ms. 87 of the Biblioteca Pública Municipal of Porto, a facsimile of which accompanies the transcription. I have also taken into account some emendations proposed by Magalhães Basto and Riley, which are indicated in the notes. My editorial criteria are conservative, in hopes that the Portuguese edition will be of use to linguists and philologists, as follows: I have resolved all abbreviations and indicated missing graphs in italics (hence "q" is rendered as "q*ue*," etc.); I have regularized i/j and u/v when used as vowels and consonants, respectively ("cavaleiro" instead of "caualeiro," etc.), and modernized accents and punctuation; I have also accentuated the second-person singular pronoun *vós* in order to distinguish it from the direct object *vos*. The notes to the Portuguese transcription are intended to be of philological or paleographical interest.

For the translation I have taken an idiomatic approach with the intention of capturing the nuances of the medieval Portuguese while at the same time making the English text flow as smoothly as possible. I have kept the explanatory notes in the translation to a minimum, my aim being to address issues of interpretation and other matters that may not be familiar to non-specialist readers in this Introduction.

Fig. 1. **Portrait of King João I of Portugal.**

Fig. 2. **The Battle of Aljubarrota.**

Fig. 3. **A medieval *wodewose*, or wild man.**

Fig. 4. **Portrait of John of Gaunt, Duke of Lancaster.**

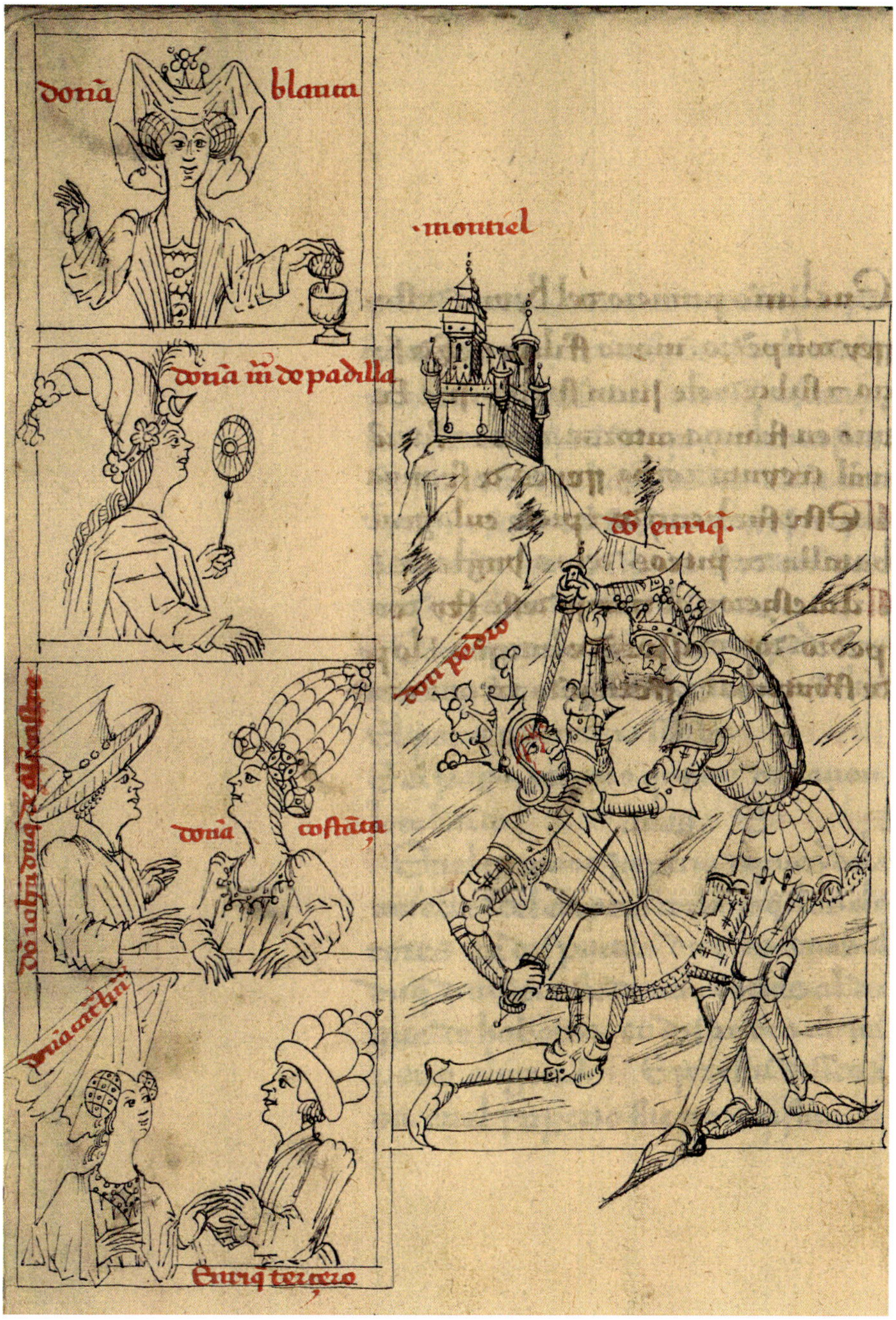

Fig. 5. **The assassination of King Pedro I of Castile, March 23, 1369.**

Fig. 6. **The Duke of Lancaster and King João I of Portugal meet at Ponte do Mouro on November 2, 1386.**

Fig. 7. **Batalha Monastery, Portugal: Recumbent funerary effigies of King João I of Portugal and Philippa of Lancaster.**

Fig. 8. **Portrait of Isabel, Duchess of Burgundy and Countess of Flanders.**

Fig. 9. **Portrait of Philip the Good, Duke of Burgundy.**

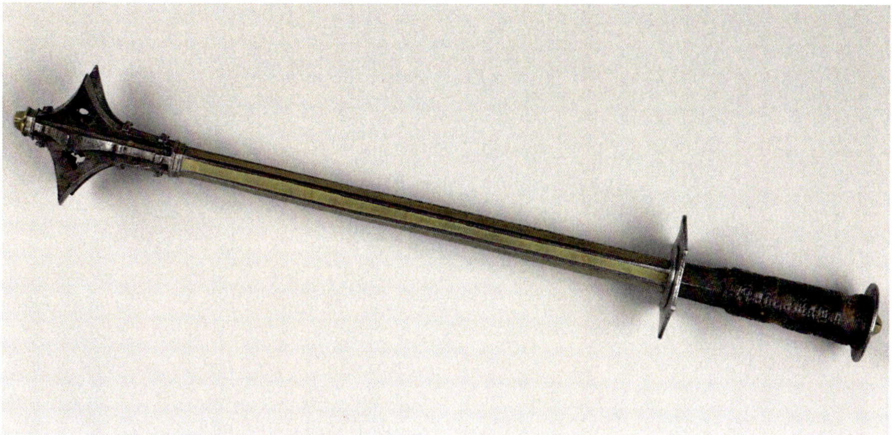

Fig. 10. **Mace, South German, ca. 1470.**

Fig. 11. **The deed of arms of the Twelve of England depicted as a tournament mêlée with lances.**

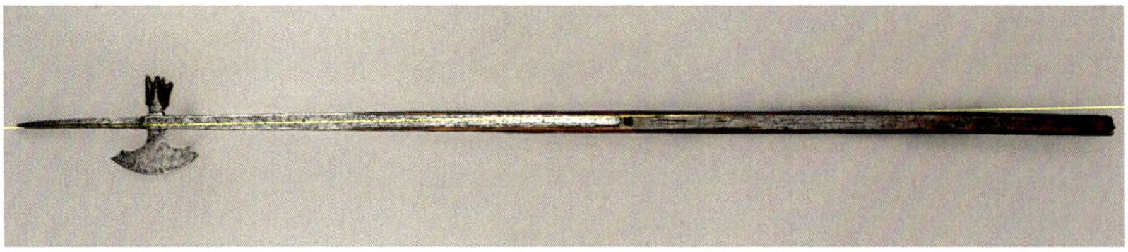

Fig. 12. **A poleaxe, probably German, ca. 1430.**

Fig. 13. **A poleaxe (detail), probably German, ca. 1430.**

Fig. 14. **War hammer with bec-de-faucon, possibly French, ca. 1450.**

Fig. 15. **Illustration of a takedown by headlock (by holding the visor; lower right).**

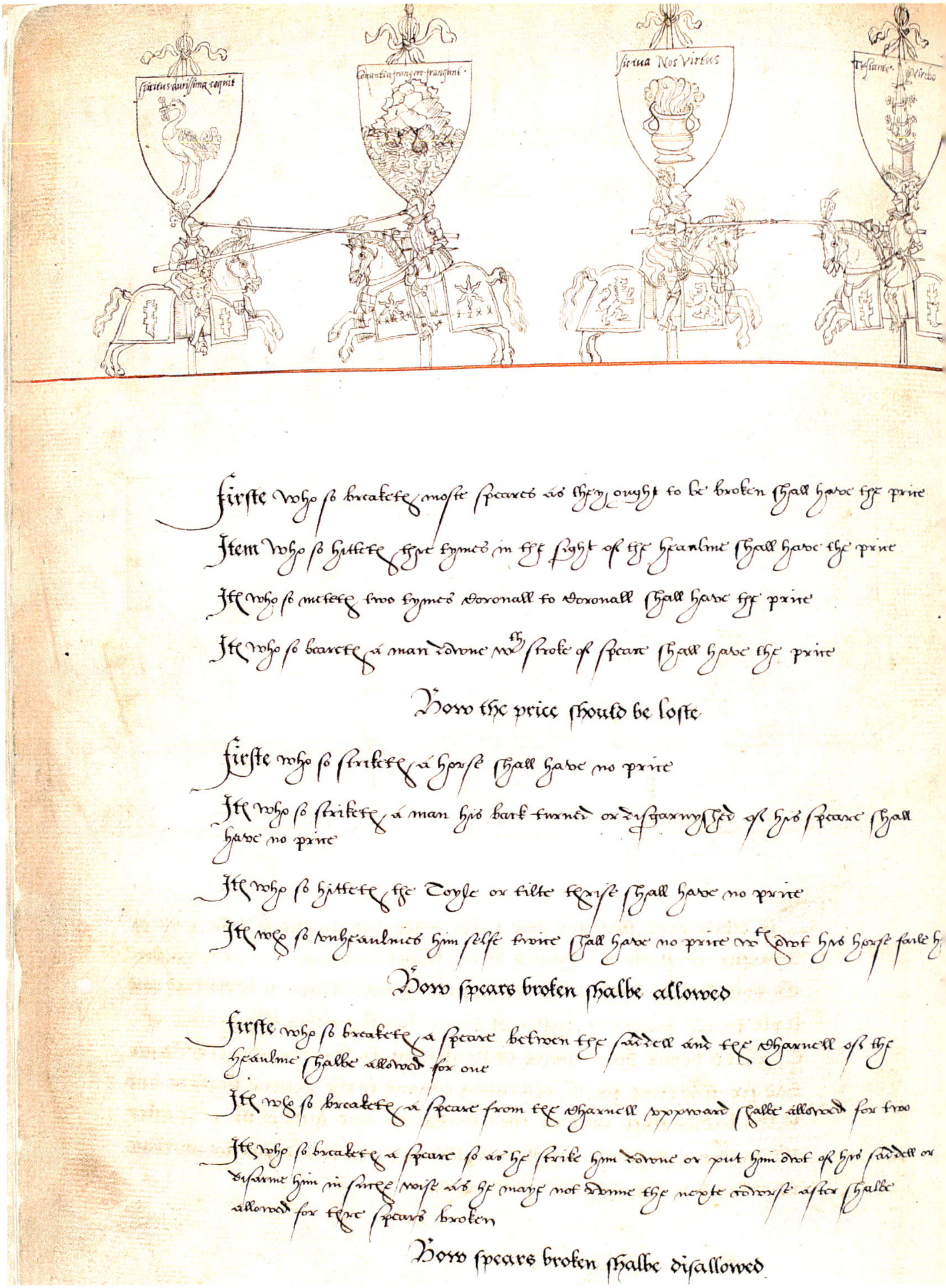

Firste who so breaketh moste speares as they ought to be broken shall have the prise

Item who so hitteth thre tymes in the sight of the heaulme shall have the prise

Ite who so meteth two tymes Coronall to Coronall shall have the prise

Ite who so beareth a man downe wt stroke of speare shall have the prise

How the price should be loste

Firste who so striketh a horse shall have no prise

Ite who so striketh a man his back turned or disarmysshed of his speare shall have no prise

Ite who so hitteth the Toyle or tilte thrise shall have no prise

Ite who so unheaulmeth him selfe twise shall have no prise wt out his horse faile h

How spears broken shalbe allowed

Firste who so breaketh a speare betwen the saddell and the charnell of the heaulme shalbe allowed for one

Ite who so breaketh a speare from the charnell upward shalbe allowed for two

Ite who so breaketh a speare so as he strike him downe or put him out of his saddell or disarme him in suche wise as he may not come the nexte course after shalbe allowed for thre speares broken

How spears broken shalbe disallowed

Fig. 16. **Lance strokes: (1) [left] to the head; (2) [right] coronal to coronal**.

57

Firste who so breaketh on the saddell shalbe disalowed for a spear breakinge

Item who so hitteth the horse or tilte once shalbe disallowed for two

Item who so hitteth the horse twice for the second tyme shalbe abated three

Item who so breaketh a speare within a foote of the coronall shalbe judged as no speare broken but a good attempte

for the price

Firste who so beareth a man downe oute of the saddell or putteth him to the earthe horse and man shall have the prize before him that striketh coronall to coronall two tymes

Item he that striketh coronall to coronall ij tymes shall have the prise before him that striketh the sight thre tymes

Item he that striketh the sight thre tymes shall have the prize before him that breaketh moste speares

Item yf there be any man that fortuneth in this wise shall be demed he bode longeste in the feld helmed and ranne the fairest course and gave the greatest strokes helpinge him selfe best with his speare &c.

Fig. 17. **Lance strokes: (3) [left] to the chest; (4) [right] making an attaint versus splintering the lance.**

Fig. 18. **Coronal with three tines of the type used in jousts of peace, ca. 1500.**

Fig. 19. **Lance points for the joust of war. Spanish, fifteenth century.**

Fig. 20. **A deed of arms ends in decapitation.**

Fig. 21. **Field armor, ca. 1420.**

Fig. 22. **The Avant armor (front view).**

Fig. 23. **The Avant armor (front, side view).**

Fig. 24. **The Avant armor (back, side view).**

Fig. 25. **Portuguese jousting helm with charnel from the royal armory of the House of Avis, ca. 1475–1500.**

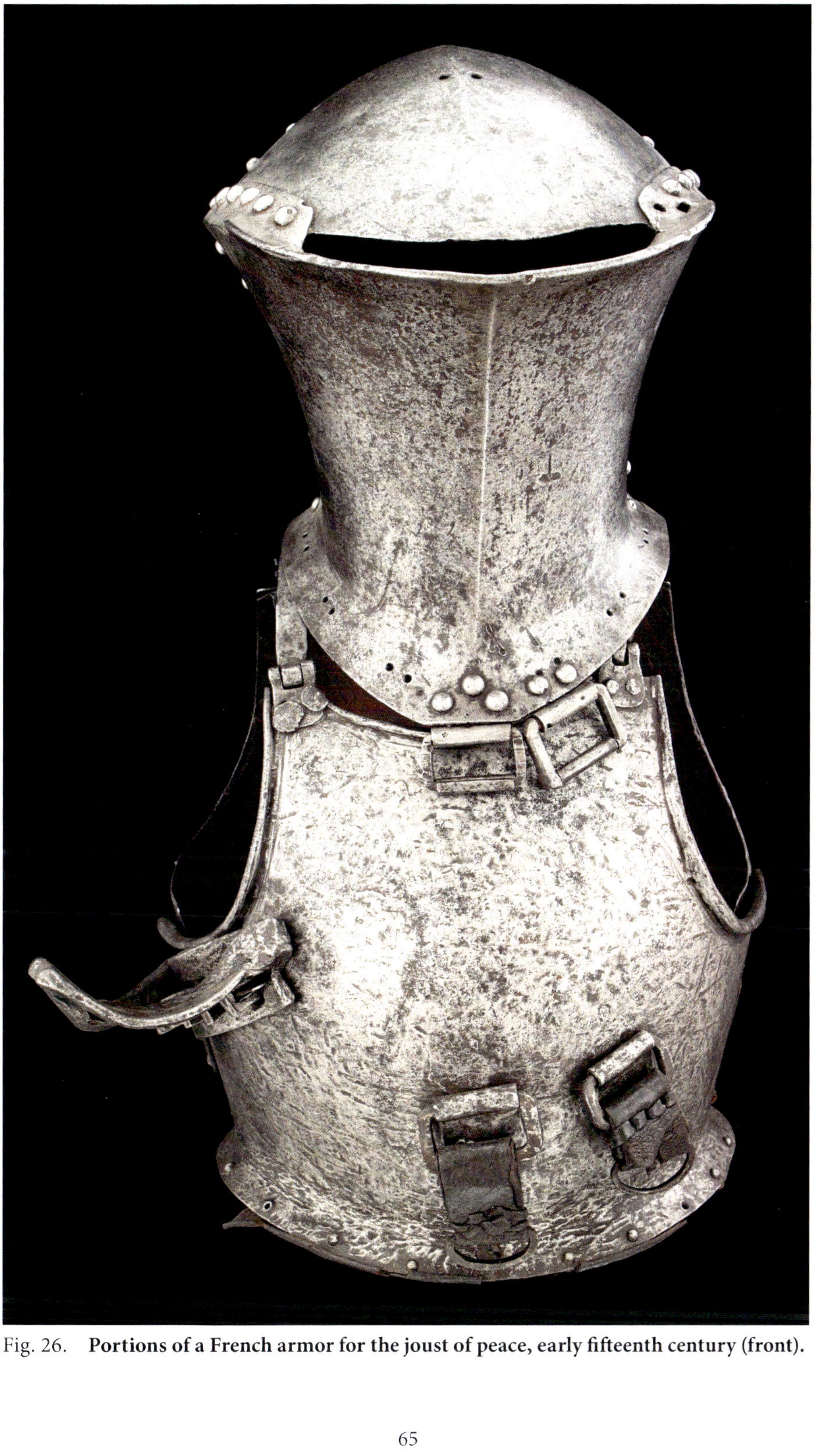

Fig. 26. **Portions of a French armor for the joust of peace, early fifteenth century (front).**

Fig. 27. **Portions of a French armor for the joust of peace, early fifteenth century (side).**

Fig. 28. **Portions of a French armor for the joust of peace, early fifteenth century (back).**

Fig. 29. **Two knights performing a deed of arms in the enclosure.**

Fig. 30. **Armet.**

4.

The Deeds of The Twelve of England: Portuguese Text

[fol. 260r] **Cavallarias de allgu*n*s fidallgos portugueses.**

Allgu*m*as cousas q*ue* fizerão o Conde d'Abranches Dom Állvaro d'Allmada, e Állvaro G*onçalvez* Magriço e outros cavalleiros portugueses em França e Basilia, e allgu*m*as em Allemanha.

Conta-sse q*ue* depois que Ell-Rei Dom João da Boa-Memória vençeo na Batalha a Ell-Rei de Castella, andando caa o Duque D'Allemcastro, com a filha do quall Ell-Rei de Portuguall era casado, que lha trouxe ao Pôrto, onde se fizerão seus solemnes esposoiros, e depois do Duque e Ell-Rei fazere*m* no reino allgu*m*as cousas, êlle se foi com[64] os seus p*ar*a Inglaterra. Onde, estando o Duque em muito contentame*n*to pella bondade q*ue* nos portugueses vira, a quem deixava sua f*ilh*a por Senhora dos quaes êlle mandou fazer em Inglaterra hu*m*a crónica das façanhas q*ue* lhe vira fazer, de q*ue* êlle era verdadeira testemunha.

[64] *com*: Written over *pa* (*para*), which has been crossed out.

Estando assi em seus sollazes, vierão os fidallguos ingreses a dizer hum dia às damas da Duquesa que erão muito feas e muito pouco p*ar*a serem damas de tam excellente senhora como a Duquesa, e, porq*ue* ellas erão desta callidade, não tinhão servidores p*ar*a que em campo lho contradissessem; do que ella[s][65] ficarão mui agastadas, e se derão por mui injuriadas, com o quall queixume se forão ao Duque e lhe pedirão que lhe[s][66] dexe cavalleiros que acudissem p*or* suas honrras e por sua parte se combatessem com os fidalguos [fol. 260v] contrários seus; e que ellas os açeitarião p*or* servidores tanto q*ue* fôssem vingadas de sua injúria, por assi aquelles doze cavalleiros os anichilarem.

Mandou então o Duque buscar allgu*ns* cavalleiros, e não se poderão achar nenhu*ns* q*ue* quisessem aceitar o campo pella vallentia dos contrários. O q*ue*, visto pello Duque, lhes disse:

"Eu, em minha côrte, não acho cavalleiros q*ue* se queirão combater co*m* vossos contrários; e porém, pois assi hé q*ue* vos não posso valler com as armas, dar-vos-ei hu*m* conselho se ho vós quiserdes. E hé q*ue*, quando eu agora vim de Portugall, em muitos recontros q*ue* Ell-Rei meu genrro ouve com hos castelhanos vi muitos e mui assinado[s][67] cavalleiros portugueses; e se vós quiserdes, eu vos nomearei doze dêstes, os melhores q*ue* eu conheço, e eu escreverei a Ell-Rei meu genrro q*ue* lhe[s][68] dê licença e lhes rogue; e se êlles quiserem tomar esta emprêsa eu tenho vosso feito por acabado. E p*ar*a isso melhor se fazer, escreva cada hu*m*a de vós sua carta a cada hum d'aquelles q*ue* por sorte vos couber; e, como vos diguo, se êlles quiserem vir, o q*ue* me pareçe q*ue* virão por sua virtude e reall cavalaria, eu vos fico q*ue* vós sereis restituídas a vossa honrra à custa de seu danno."

E, beijando ellas as mãos ao Duque, lhe disserão q*ue* erão mui contentes; e fazendo logo o Duque os nomes dos caval*ei*ros, cada hum em seu papell, lançando sortes, tomou cada hu*m*a o q*ue* lhe aconteçeo e coube à sua parte de man*ei*ra

---

65 *ella[s]*: *ella* in the manuscript.

66 *lhe pedirão que lhes*: The manuscript reads *lhes pedirão que lhe.*

67 *assinado[s]*: *assinado* in the manuscript.

68 *lhe[s]*: *lhe* in the manuscript.

q*ue* p*or* o nome soube cada hu*m*a das damas quall era ho seu cavalleiro, a q*ue* cada hu*m*a particullarm*ente* escreveo, em q*ue* lhe rogava e pedia q*ue*, pello q*ue* devião à cavallaria, ouvessem p*or* bem de as virem tirar de tamanha afronta. E o Duque, por sua via, escreveo a Ell-Rei pedindo-lhe muito q*ue* lho rogasse a êlles escrevendo-lhes também a elles juntamente hu*m*a carta em que lhes pedia q*ue*, por amor dêlle e pollo q*ue* devião à Ordem da [fol. 261r] Cavallaria, quisessem açeitar aquella emprêsa por cada hu*m*a d'aquellas damas; porque dellas selhe segueria grande honrra, fama e louvor por êlle não achar em sua côrte cavalleiros q*ue* por sua parte dellas o quisessem açeitar.

Ao q*ue* êlles responderão q*ue*, avida licença dell-Rei seu senhor, êlles serião em Inglaterra o Pentecoste seguinte, que era o dia do prazo. A quall l*icen*ça deu loguo Ell-Rei aos cavalleiros, q*ue* se diz serem da Serra da Estrêlla, d'aquelles lugares q*ue* estão pella frallda da serra como Trancoso, Pinhell. Os quaes cavalleiros erão: o q*ue* depois foi Conde d'Abranches, en França, Do*m* Állvaro d'Almada; e Állvaro G*onçal*v*e*z Magriço; e hum Pacheco; e Pedromem; e outros, q*ue* erão por todos doze; todos home*n*s espeçiaes em feitos d'armas, e experimentados.

Os quaes partirão e se forão à çidade do Pôrto, e hos onze tomarão hu*m*a nao e embarcarão nella e partirão d'alli p*ara* Inglaterra. Állvaro G*onçal*v*e*z Magriço quis hir p*or* terra desenfadando-sse e p*or* ver allgu*m*as cousas pello caminho, p*ro*metendo-lhes q*ue* se êlle não morresse, q*ue* êlle seria com êlles ao prazo limitado.

Partidos os da não com próspero vento, aportarão na cidade de Londres, onde forão bem reçebidos e festejados das damas do Duque.

E a êste tempo falleçia mais de dous dias p*ara* o prazo da batalha e não vinha Állvaro G*onçal*v*e*z; e, de quam allegres estavão as onze com os seus cav*a*l*e*iros, tam triste estava aquella a que*m* o dito Állvaro G*onçal*v*e*z coubera, dizendo mall assi p*or* ella ser a mais malave*n*turada na tardança de seu cavalleiro, e q*ue* nella avia de cahir a sorte de não vir e falleçer, como lhe pareçia, pella batalha estar já tam perto. A esto lhe responderão q*ue* não se agastasse porque êlle era tall cavalleiro q*ue*, se morte lho não estrovasse, êlle viria a tempo q*ue* comprisse com o q*ue* prometera; e que, quando a ventura quisesse q*ue* não viesse, q*ue* êlles onze se combaterião com os doze ingreses, e assi ella [fol. 261v] seria a mais ditosa porq*ue* por seu respeito allcançarião môr honrra e fama.

Passando entre êlles e ellas estas e outras práticas, ex q*ue* chega Állvaro G*onçalvez*, de q*ue* todos forão mui ledos; e assi todos doze, como estavão, se forão ao Duque, ao quall disserão q*ue* êlles erão alli vindos a seu rôgo p*ara* se poerem a aquelle trançe; e que, porqua*n*to êlles erão cavalleiros estrangeiros e q*ue* não tinhão coostas de ninguém, e os cavalleiros com quem êlles avião de combater erão naturaes e na terra grandes senhores, q*ue* poderia ser q*ue*, dando-lhes a ventura com êlles vitória, q*ue* os tratarião mall, q*ue* sua senhoria os segurasse.

O Duque chamou os doze cavalleiros ingreses e lhes disse q*ue* aquelles cavalleiros erão os cometedores dêste desafio, e q*ue* aquell'outros erão os q*ue* as damas apresentavão p*or* si; e que àquelles cavalleiros, se caso fôsse q*ue* êlles os vençessem, q*ue* lhes não fôsse feito nenhu*m* desaguisado—por si nem por seus parentes—, e que êlle os tomava sôbre sua cabeça; q*ue* soubessem q*ue* se allgu*m*a cousa se fizesse, q*ue* a êlle seria feita, e q*ue* castigaria mui rijo aquelles q*ue* o tall fizessem ou cometessem assi como se contra sua p*esso*a fôsse cometida. E êlles então responderão q*ue* êlles o seguravão e que não ouvessem reçeo de nada.

Acabado isto, e chegando-sse o dia da batalha, ao tempo de entrar nella reçebeo cada hum dos portugueses de cada dama seu joel[69] e cada hu*m*a o lançou ao pescoço ao seu cavalleiro; e assi os meterão no campo, hindo todos a pee armados de ponto em branco.

E os juízes os meterão no campo, estando o Duque e tôda a cidade de Londres em grandes cadafallssos dos quaes a Duquesa com suas damas vião a batalha q*ue* doze por doze fazião; na quall entravão sôbre o motivo q*ue* já disse: q*ue* as damas erão m*ui*to feas e de muito mao pareçer e q*ue* não erão boas q*ue* nesta demanda achassem cavalleiros q*ue* lhe ousassem contradizer o q*ue* dezião, o q*ue* em campo donde estavão [fol. 262r] o farião conheçer a quem lho contradissesse.

---

[69] *seu ioel*: The manuscript reads *seu joel ioel*, with *joel* crossed out; this is a common scribal error known in the field of paleography as dittography. See also below, notes 70 and 79.

A esto responderão os portugueses q*ue* as senhoras erão damas, tam gentiis molheres e tam fermosas q*ue*, por suas gentilezas, mereçião q*ue* cavalleiros de mui estranhas terras as viessem servir e morrer p*or* seu serviço, como êlles farião se êlles lho contradissessem.

E sôbre estas palavras começarão sua batalha com suas maças de ferro, a quall cometerão com tamanho ímpetu e sanha que, começando-sse pella manham, andarão ta*n*to q*ue* às horas da Têrça, por aprazime*n*to de todos, descanssarão.

E, acabando de tomar allgum ta*n*to repouso, tornarão à sua batalha, onde se os portugueses meterão com[70] seus contrários com tamanho ímpetu e viguor finalme*n*te q*ue* ficarão oito dêlles mui mall, e lançando todo fora do campo ficarão êlles vençedores. E perguntando aos juízes se tinhão mais q*ue* fazer p*ar*a q*ue* aquellas senhoras fôssem restituídas na honrra q*ue* mereçião, q*ue* aquelles cavalleiros querião menosgabar, êlles lhe[s][71] disserão q*ue* não. E assi com muita honrra e louvor se sahírão do campo e se forão descanssar a hu*m*a casa q*ue* para isso estava ordenada, onde loguo vierão as damas e o Duque. E já vedes a allegria q*ue* estas senhoras terião.

Assentados a mesa p*ar*a tomar refeição do trabalho passado, tomarão as damas águoa p*ar*a lançarem aas mãos, cada hu*m*a a seu cavalleiro; e quando a dama d'Állvaro G*onçalvez* Magriço lhe quis lançar ágoa às mãos, êlle não consentio. E pondo as mãos detraas lhe disse:

"Senhora, nenhu*m*a molher me lançou ágoa às mãos neste mundo, e p*or* isso não consentirei q*ue* vós mo façaes."

E ella, apertando com êlle q*ue* o quisesse consentiir, lhe disse q*ue*, pois as outras senhoras o fizerão assi, cada huma ao seu cavall*ei*ro, q*ue* ella em tôda a man*e*ira lha avia de lançar. O q*ue* êlle, vendo, lhe disse:

"Não refusava eu a mer[fol. 262v]çê p*or* me não achar p*or* muito honrrado com ella; mas a pouca dignidade e merecime*n*tos de minha pessoa, e o ter mãos tam cheas de cabellos me fazião não na açeitar. Mas, pois assi hé, que quem

---

[70] *com*: *com com* in the manuscript.

[71] *lhe[s]*: *lhe* in the manuscript.

pode mandar, eu, como súbdito e vosso servidor quero obedeçer. E isto eu o encubro, como vedes, senhora, q*ue* a Natureza obrou tam mall comigo q*ue* atee às unhas me deu os cabellos."

Respondeo ella:

"Senhor, antes essas vossas mãos são eu obrigada beijar e lavar muitas vezes, e fazer-lhe todo o acatamento, pois q*ue* por ellas sou livre d'aquella infâmia q*ue* aquelles caval*ei*ros me querião poer; e pois ellas me livrarão, justa cousa hé q*ue* a que*m* tamanha [cousa][72] vós com ellas fizestes vo-llas beije."

Então[73] consentio Állvaro G*onçal*v*e*z q*ue* lha desse. A assi se poserão à mesa. E depois de comerem e descanssarem andarão na côrte allgu*n*s dias. Onde, lhe veio ter às orelhas que os cavalleiros ingreses, achando-sse injuriados do passado, determinavão com gentes os matarem, depois q*ue* fôssem sãos; o q*ue*, sabudo p*or* êlles, pedirão l*icen*ça ao Duque, e êlle lha deu, e se punha p*or* êlles, dizendo q*ue* fôssem seguros porq*ue* em sua terra se lhe não faria agravo nem desacato, o quall lhe tiverão em merçê. E beijando-lhe as mãos se despedirão.

E dêstes doze cavalleiros ficarão três naquellas partes e os nove se vierão p*ar*a Portugall, honde hum d'aquelles, q*ue* depois foi Conde d'Abranches, fêz taes cousas em França q*ue* o fêz Conde naquella parte d'Abranches. E este Conde hé o q*ue* morreo na Alfarrobeira quando Ell-Rei Dom Affonsso o Quinto ouve batalha com o I*nffan*te Dom P*edr*o, seu tio e sogro; na quall também o dito I*nffan*te foi morto, ao quall disse o I*nffan*te quando vio tantos da parte dell-Rei ao Conde:

"Hã! Conde! Q*ue* faremos?"

E êlle respondeo aquella notávell pallavra:

"Senn*h*or, jantar aqui e hir cear ao inferno!"

Assi q*ue* dêste não sabemos os feitos q*ue* fêz em França [fol. 263r] especificadame*n*te.

---

72 *[cousa]*: Not in the manuscript. Riley, *Os Doze de Inglaterra: Ficção e Realidade*, p. 32, conjectures that the amanuensis skipped a word when copying the text, and suggests adding *cousa*. Omission of a word, or haplography, is a common scribal error so Riley's theory is a sound one, especially since the sentence makes more sense as emended.

73 *Então*: The manuscript reads *Então elle*, with *elle* crossed out.

Állvaro d'Allmada—êste o q*ue* atrás ch*a*ma Conde d'Abranches[74]—se foi à Allemanha e, na cidade de Basilia, ouve hum gram desafio com hu*m* allemão. E o conçêrto era armas p*or* armas, taes p*or* taes, sob penna de ser alleivoso e de nunqua mais tomar armas e de ser alleivoso, como diguo, o q*ue* não cumprisse.

Entrarão estes cavalleiros em campo e começarão hu*m*a brava batalha entre ambos q*ue* era maravilha de ver. E trazendo o português malltratado o allemão, e vendo-sse já perdido e quási vençido, tirou de hum bastão q*ue* trazia, e ficoulhe hu*m* garfo d'açeiro, e lancou-lho a hum hombro e desguarneçeo ho arnês a Állvaro d'Allmada,[75] e levava-lhe no garfo carne da espádoa. Quando Állvaro d'Allmada vio o gancho e como de hu*m*a soo vez lhe despedaçara o arnês e parte das carnes, lançando a bisarma no chão e remetendo a êlle, com tamanha fúria lhe apertou a garganta e deu com êlle no chão e alli leixou o fôllego prim*ei*ro q*ue* si allevantasse.

E vendo o Emperador a treição do allemão e como usara de treedor em não cumprir os pontos com q*ue* entrarão no campo, ouve Állvaro d'Almada p*or* bom cavalleiro e ao allemão p*or* treedor.

Quanto a Állvaro G*onçal*v*e*z, o q*ue* fêz hé o seguinte.

Acabada a batalha em Inglaterra, Állvaro G*onçal*v*e*z Magriço se passou a Frandes e foi-sse a casa do Conde, q*ue* era casado com Madam Isabell, q*ue* era filha dell-Rei de Portugall, Dom João de Boa-Memória.

E andando em sua casa vierão embaixadores dell-Rei de França p*ar*a o dito Conde de Frandes, os quaes dezião, da parte dell-Rei de França, q*ue* êlle queria fazer Côrtes, q*ue* fôsse a ellas como devia e era obrigado; do q*ue* a Condessa foi muito espa*n*tada e disse ao Conde:

"E! Bem, Se*n*n*h*or! Às Côrtes dell-Rei de França sois vós obrigado de hir?"

---

[74] êste *o que atrás chama Conde d'Abranches*: Written in the margin in the same hand as the manuscript.

[75] *d'Allmada*: The manuscript has *Glz* crossed out and corrected. The copyist momentarily confused Álvaro d'Almada and Álvaro Gonçalvez and corrected the mistake.

[fol. 263v] E êlle lhe disse que si, q*ue* seu pai e seus avóos sempre tiverão essa obrigação, em comprime*n*to da quall hião a ellas quando erão requeridos, e q*ue* por isso não podia all fazer senão fazer o q*ue* êlles fizerão pella obrigação q*ue* tinhão. Ao q*ue* ella respondeo q*ue* lhe pesava m*u*ito de aquella sogeição e q*ue* ella o tinha a maa ventura e q*ue* se tinha p*or* cativa; e porém q*ue* ella p*ro*metia, como f*ilh*a de quem era, q*ue* ella se afforrasse dell-Rei de França, dêlle nem ella hirem àas suas Côrtes.

Disse então o Duque:

"Isso, Senhora, não se pode fazer, porq*ue* vem já p*or* descende*n*tes e não se pode cobra[r][76] p*or* ser como hé, de justiça e direito q*ue* Ell-Rei de França neste condado tem."

Disse ella então:

"Vós, S*e*nn*h*or, não hireis laa, senão eu."

E, para comprime*n*to desta p*ro*messa, com muito brevidade se enderençou e se partio para Parys, onde as Côrtes se fazião, e mandou poer hu*m*a cadeira iguall com a dell-Rei de França na quall se assentou. E quando os prinçipaes de França assi a virão, "S*e*nn*h*or, não abasta ao Conde de Frandes não vir a as vossas Cortes," disserão êlles, "Mas antes, sendo [vosso vassalo][77] como forão todos os Duques de Borgonha seu[s][78] anteçessores, mas o Duque Dom Fillipe manda poer cadeira de sua molher iguall com a vossa."

Disse[79] então alli à Condessa:

"E por que não vinha o Duque, vosso marido? Não sabe êlle q*ue* o seu[80] Condado e Ducado de Frandes e Borgonha forão sempre os duques dêlles obrigados a vir a ellas?"

---

76 *cobra[r]*: *cobra* in the manuscript.

77 *[vosso vassalo]*: Not in the manuscript. The emendation is suggested by Magalhães Basto and Costa, *Relação ou Crónica breve das cavalarias dos Doze de Inglaterra*, p. 98, and Magalhães Basto, *O essencial sobre Os Doze de Inglaterra*, p. 38. This is possibly another case of haplography. I have followed the suggested emendation, for the sake of clarity.

78 *seu[s]*: *seu* in the manuscript.

79 *Disse*: The manuscript reads *Disse disse*.

80 *seu*: The manuscript reads *seum*.

Ao que ella respondeo:

"Senn*h*or, o Duque não vem porq*ue* eu soo aqui apareço p*or* êlle, e digo q*ue* vós não tendes direito em constrangerdes ao Duque que venha a vossas Côrtes, e a razão [é][81] porq*ue*, se vós quiserdes q*ue* por armas se determine, eu darei cavalleiro q*ue* se combata com outro vosso q*ue* o Duque e eu e todos os nossos descendentes sejão livres de nunqua vir a vossas Côrtes, e se o vosso vençer q*ue* a terra fique obrigada como dizeis, e atee'qui foi. Porque quando eu casei com ho Duque, não soube desta sogeição q*ue* dizeis que tem, porque não consentira q*ue* filha de tamanho Rei [fol. 264r] como eu são casara com home*m* sogeito."

Quando Ell-Rei de França vio a demanda da Duquesa e Condessa, que era porque tinha na sua côrte cavalleiros mui aprovados em feitos d'armas, os quaes não desejavão outro bem senão cousas em q*ue* exerçitassem seus esforços, sahío loguo hum mui vallente cavalleiro françês e pedio p*or* merçê a Ell-Rei q*ue* lhe outorgasse aquella emprêsa, a quall Ell-Rei lhe conçedeo porq*ue* sabia de sua vale*n*tia e esfôrço que nas armas tinha. E poserão logo prazo q*ue* dahí a hum mês ella mandasse o seu caval*ei*ro p*ar*a se combatere*m* ambos.

Isto acabado, a Duquesa se tornou a Frandes.

Deixemos[82] as razões q*ue* teve com Ell-Rei de França sôbre o poer da cadeira, ca disse q*ue* lhe pertençia, por ser como era, filha de tam famoso Rei, e vollta, como digo, a Frandes deu co*n*ta ao Duque do negóçio como ficara, e êlle a reprehendeo, dizendo:

"Q*ue* p*ar*a que era mataren-sse os home*n*s em desafio?"

Finallme*n*te, q*ue* buscando e rogando ella muito, nunqua achou nenhu*m* framengo q*ue* quisesse açeitar o desafio, porq*ue* avião que não tinha justiça. E qua*n*do a Duquesa vio que em Frandes se não achavão que*m* o quisesse aceitar

81 *[é]*: Not in the manuscript. I once again follow the emendation suggested by Magalhães Basto and Costa, *Relação ou Crónica breve das cavalarias dos Doze de Inglaterra*, p. 99, and Magalhães Basto, *O essencial sobre Os Doze de Inglaterra*, p. 39.

82 *Deixemos*: *A deixemos* in the manuscript. Riley, *Os Doze de Inglaterra: Ficção e Realidade*, p. 34, n. 1, conjectures that the error may be due to the fact that the amanuensis inadevertently skipped a line of the text from which he was copying. This was certainly a common type of error, known in the field of paleography as homœoteleuton, so Riley's theory is plausible.

disse q*ue* alli estava Állvaro G*onçalvez* Magriço, que era criado dell-Rei seu pai, q*ue* êlle se combateria p*or* sua parte com ho cavalleiro françês. E quando o Duque vio q*ue* ella assi ensistia, disse q*ue* se chamasse Állvaro G*onçalvez*. E vindo êlle, preguntou ho Conde se queria entrar p*or* sua parte naquella batalha; e êlle lhe respondeo q*ue* si.

E perguntando-lhe o Duque e Conde[83] q*ue* teúdo era q*ue* avia mester para aquelle auto, e êlle lhe disse q*ue* se êlle tivesse na côrte dell-Rei de França allgum amigo no quall se estrevesse q*ue* lhe daria o neçessário, q*ue* o enderençasse a êlle, q*ue* laa se prove[fol. 264v]ria do que avia mester; e que p*ara* êlle lhe desse, como deu, cartas p*ara* hum Conde, grande amigo do Duque Fillipe, na quall lhe pedia q*ue* de tudo neçessário o prouvesse, porqua*n*to hia poer-sse em armas por sua parte, e lhe desse todo o bom aviame*n*to.

Com estas cartas se partio Állvaro G*onçalvez* vestido em hábitos de romeiro, com seu bordão na mão e com hu*m*a roupa çarrada, na quall levava a carta. E assi, hindo p*or* êsse caminho, quasi mendicando, aportou em Parys, onde estava Ell-Rei de França, e tôda a sua corte, esperando o prazo p*ara* verem o desafio.

E tanto q*ue* em Parys foi, foi-sse à casa do Conde, e pedindo esmola acertou o Conde de chegar a hu*m*a janella; e sabendo q*ue* era aquelle, lhe disse que lhe queria dar, como deu, hu*m*a carta.

E vista p*or* êlle lhe disse:

"Sois vós o cavalleiro?"

Disse Állvaro G*onçalvez*:

"Senn*h*or, si, e venho neste hábito p*or* se não saber quem são."

"Agora de manham," disse o Conde, "q*ue* se compre o derradeiro dia do prazo."

"Si," disse Állvaro G*onçalvez*, "E vos peço muito p*or* merçê, e por aquello q*ue* deveis à Ordem da Cavallaria, e pella amizade q*ue* tendes com ho Duque meu senhor, p*or* êlle ser, como hé, muito vosso amigo, q*ue* nesse estrevimento

---

[83] *perguntando-lhe o Duque e Conde*: Preceded by *perguntoulhe o Duque e Conde*, which is crossed out.

me mandou assinadamente a vós q*ue* vós me desenganeis dando-me armas e cavallo desenganados p*ar*a entrar neste desafio."

A q*ue* o Conde respondeo q*ue* êlle o faria, de man*e*ira q*ue* per sua pr*ó*pria pessoa faria experiênçia. E mandando per hu*m*as armas e cavallo, êlle as prouvou e achou muito boas, as quaes vestio Állvaro G*onçalvez*. E cavalgando no cavallo, hindo assi muito bem armado, era já tarde e a gente era tanta pellos muros e pallanques q*ue* era maravilha.

E o françês, que avia já vinte e nove dias, quando veio ao dia do prazo em q*ue* êlle se pôs e andou armado, vendo que [fol. 265r] era já mui tarde e q*ue* lhe não sahía ninguém, de sôldo e soberbo começou de pedir em alltas vozes estromentos de como alli viera sem achar pessoa da parte do Duque Fillipe p*ar*a q*ue* com êlle se combatesse.

Estando nisto, entra no campo Állvaro G*onçalvez*, e começou a andar apallpa*n*do o campo e a olhá-llo muito.

O françês, q*ue* já estava à po*n*to, quando vio q*ue* o Portuguese gastava mais o tempo e*m* andar a redor do campo, pareçendo-lhe q*ue* de covarde e temeroso o fazia, e também porq*ue* passara p*or* junto dêlle duas ou três vezes correndo as estâncias sem lhe fallar, lhe disse allto q*ue* geralme*n*te se ouvio:

"Eu nunqua vi tam riballdo cavalleiro! E segundo mostra em seu pouco esfôrço, allgu*m* polltron velho deve de ser pois se escusa ta*n*to de combater comiguo."

Ao quall Állvaro G*onçalvez* respondeo:

"Vós, Dom Caval*e*iro, mentis pella gorja! E por isso me matarei convosco e vos farei conheçer q*ue* sou melhor caval*e*iro que vós."

E arremetendo ambos com gram fortalleza hu*m* p*ar*a o outro, tamanhos encontros se derão q*ue*, juntamente, cavallos e senhores vierão a terra, e com muita presteza se levantarão, e vierão à batalha das espadas, a quall durou p*or* mui grande espaço, não se*m* muita admiração dell-Rei e sua côrte.

Finallmente, Állvaro G*onçalvez* se ouve com tanta fortalleza[84] com o françês q*ue* no cabo da batalha ho vençeo e cortou a cabeça.

---

[84] *fortalleza*: Preceded by the word *esforço*, which has been crossed out.

E dalli foi recolhido por allguns amigos do Duque e foi-sse p*ar*a êlle.

E desta man*e*ira livrou Állvaro G*onçalvez* Magriço, a rôgo de Madama, o Condado de Frandes da sogeição de França p*ar*a sempre—ao quall forão feitas grandes honrras e merçês.

E após isso, querendo-sse êlle vir a Portuguall, escreverão a Ell-Rei Dom João da Boa-Memória q*ue* [fol. 265v] fizesse muita honrra e merçê a aquelle cavalleiro porq*ue* posera em liberdade o Condado de Frandes e o livrara d'aquella sogeição de França; e Ell-Rei, p*or* satisfação de tamanha cousa, lhe fêz muita merçê e o fêz Conde[85] e foi o fundame*n*to da casa sua.

E destas cousas há hí crónica em Inglaterra q*ue* largamente trata dêstes cavalleiros e dos grandes feitos d'armas q*ue* la fizerão.

---

[85] *Conde*: Followed by a lacuna in the manuscript.

5.
The Deeds of The Twelve of England: English Translation

Deeds of Arms of Some Portuguese Noblemen.

Some deeds that the Count of Avranches, Dom Álvaro de Almada, and Álvaro Gonçalves Magriço, and other Portuguese knights performed in France and Basel, and other deeds in Germany.

The story goes that after King Dom João of Happy Memory vanquished the king of Castile in the Battle, the Duke of Lancaster—to whose daughter the King of Portugal was married, having brought her to Porto where they took their solemn marital vows—was traveling in Portugal and, after the Duke and the King had taken care of some business in the kingdom, the Duke left with his retinue for England. At that time, as he was very pleased about the goodness he had seen in the Portuguese, to whom he had entrusted his daughter as their Lady, he ordered a chronicle to be made in England about the deeds that he had seen them perform, of which he was a faithful witness.

One day, while the Duchess' ladies were taking their ease, some English noblemen came and told them that they were very ugly and of too low a class to be the ladies of such an excellent woman as the Duchess, and, because they were of this quality, they would not have vassals who would dare prove the English noblemen wrong in the enclosure. The ladies were very vexed about this, and they took great umbrage and went to the Duke with their complaint and requested that he provide them with knights who would uphold their honor and fight on their behalf with the noblemen who were against them; and they would accept them as vassals until such time as they were avenged for their insult, for which those twelve knights would annihilate them.

Thus the Duke ordered some knights to be sought out, and none could be found who would dare accept the challenge because of the valor of the opponents. When this was witnessed by the Duke, he said to the ladies:

"I cannot find knights in my own court who are willing to fight against your enemies; and therefore, since I cannot avail with arms, I shall give you a piece of advice if you should wish it. And it is this: I recently returned from Portugal, where in many encounters that my son-in-law the King had with the Castilians I saw a great deal of very redoubtable Portuguese knights; and if you should wish, I shall nominate twelve of them, the best ones that I know, and I shall write to my son-in-law the King so that he may grant them license and beseech them; and if they should wish to undertake this emprise I shall consider your case settled. And in order the better to do this, write a letter, each one of you, to each one whose lot you draw; and, as I say, if they should wish to come, which I believe they will because of their virtue and unerring chivalry, I assure you that you will be restored to your honor at the cost of the Englishmen's harm."

And, kissing the Duke's hands, the ladies told him that they were most content. And then the Duke wrote the name of each knight on separate pieces of paper, shuffled them, and each lady took the one that by chance fell to her lot, so that each one of the ladies knew who her knight was by name. The ladies each wrote letters to their respective knights in which they besought and asked them that, for all they owed to chivalry, they see fit to come and deliver them from such an enormous affront. And the Duke, for his part, wrote to the King asking him to beseech them in earnest. He himself wrote a letter to them as well at the same time to request that, for love of him and all that they owed the Order of Chivalry, they accept that emprise for each one of the ladies; because of whom great honor, fame and praise would follow the knights, for the Duke had been unable to find in his own court any knights who would dare accept on the ladies' behalf.

To this the Portuguese knights replied that, after being granted license by the King, their Lord, they would be in England the following Pentecost, which was the day of the deadline. The King then granted this license to the knights, whom it is said are from the Mountain Range of the Star, from places that are at the foot of the mountain range, like Trancoso and Pinhel. The knights in question were: Dom Álvaro de Almada, who was later the Count of Avranches, in France; and Álvaro Gonçalves Magriço; and a certain Pacheco; and Pedro Homem; and some others, twelve in all; each one of them skilled and experienced in feats of arms.

The Portuguese knights departed and made their way to the city of Porto, and eleven of them took a ship and embarked in it and departed thence for England. Álvaro Gonçalves Magriço wished to go by land at a leisurely pace and see some things along the way, promising them that, so long as he did not die, he would be with them by the established deadline.

Those in the ship having departed with a favorable wind, they came to port at the city of London, where they were well received and fêted by the Duke's ladies.

And at this time just two days remained before the deadline for the battle, and Álvaro Gonçalves still had not arrived; and, as glad as the eleven ladies were with their knights, as sad was she who had drawn the name of Álvaro Gonçalves, cursing thus for being the most unfortunate lady because of the tardiness of her knight, and that it was just her luck to have picked the name of the one who would fail to arrive on time, so it seemed to her, because the day of the battle was now so close. At this point they told her not to be upset for he was such a knight that, so long as death did not prevent him, he would come in time to fulfill his promise; and that, if fortune wished that he not come, the eleven of them would fight against the twelve Englishmen, and she would therefore be the happiest because on her behalf they would achieve greater honor and fame.

While these and other conversations were taking place between the men and women, here came Álvaro Gonçalves, which made them all very merry; and thus all twelve, as they were now there, went to the Duke, to whom they said that they had come there at his request in order to take part in that duel. Also, since they were foreign knights and had no resources from anyone else, and the knights with whom they were to fight were native inhabitants and great lords of the land, and since it could turn out that good fortune would grant victory to the Portuguese and they would be badly treated, they entreated his lordship to guarantee them a safe-conduct.

The Duke called over the twelve English knights and told them that they were the challengers of this duel, and that the others were the ones that the ladies were presenting on their behalf; and that, in the event that the Portuguese vanquished the English, no offense would be committed against those knights—neither by the English knights themselves nor by members of their families—and that he held the Portuguese knights in high esteem. And they should know that if they did do anything, it would be the same as doing it to him, and he would punish those who did or committed such a deed very harshly, as if it had been committed against his own person. And the English knights then responded that they gave him their safe-conduct and that the Portuguese should not fear a thing.

This done, and the day of the battle having arrived, as they were getting ready to fight, each one of the Portuguese men received from each lady her jewel, and each lady hung it around the neck of her knight; and thus did they place them in the enclosure, all of them going on foot, armed at all points in white armor.

And the judges placed them in the enclosure, and the Duke and all the city of London were standing on great platforms from which the Duchess with her ladies could see the battle that twelve would do against twelve, which they were entering into because of the charge already stated about the ladies being very ugly and highly unseemly and not pretty enough to find knights for this suit who would dare try to prove wrong what the Englishmen had said, and that, in the enclosure where they now were, the Englishmen would make it known to anyone who would dare try to prove them wrong.

To this the Portuguese replied that the women were ladies, such kind women, and so beautiful that, for their kindnesses, they deserved that knights from far-off lands come to serve them and die in their service, as the English knights would if they tried to prove them wrong.

And with these words they commenced their battle with their iron maces, in which they engaged with such great ferocity and fury that, having begun in the morning, they continued for so long that during the hours of Tierce, to everyone's relief, they rested.

And, after they had finished taking a rest for a while, they returned to their battle, where the Portuguese attacked their enemies with such ferocity and vigor that finally eight of them were in very bad shape; and after throwing all of the Englishmen out of the enclosure the Portuguese were the victors. And asking the judges if there was anything else that needed to be done in order for the women to be restored to the honor that they deserved, whom those knights wished to scorn, the judges told them that there was not. And so the Portuguese knights left the enclosure with great honor and praise and went to rest at a palace that had been arranged for this purpose, where they then saw the ladies and the Duke. And you can imagine how happy these women were.

When the men were seated at table for the banquet in the wake of their endeavor, the ladies took water to splash on their hands, each one to her knight; and when Álvaro Gonçalves Magriço's lady went to splash water on his hands, he would not allow it. And putting his hands behind him he said:

"My lady, no woman in this world ever splashed water on my hands, and for this reason I shall not allow you to do so."

And she insisted that he allow it, telling him that, since the other women had done so, each one to her knight, she had to splash in exactly the same way. On seeing this he said to her:

"I was not refusing her ladyship because I do not consider myself to be most honored by her; rather the slight worth and merits of my person, and my having hands so covered in hair were making me unable to accept. But, since the saying goes that she who can, commands, I, as your subject and vassal, am compelled to obey! And I cover this up, as you can see, my lady, because Nature worked so badly on me that she gave me hair right up to my nails."

She replied:

"Sire, on the contrary, I am obliged to kiss and wash these hands of yours many times, and to pay you every respect, since because of them I am delivered from that infamy into which those knights wished to thrust me; and since these hands delivered me, it is a just thing that, for such a great deed that you performed with them, I kiss them."

Then Álvaro Gonçalves allowed her to kiss his hand. And so they sat at table. And after they had eaten and rested they spent a few days at court. During this time it came to their attention that the English knights, considering themselves insulted after what had happened, had determined with some men to kill them after they had recuperated; and once the Portuguese found out about this, they begged license of the Duke, and he granted it, and he argued forcefully on their behalf, saying that they had been granted safe-conduct so that in his land no harm or discourtesy would be done to them, for which they had acknowledged his beneficence. And kissing his hands they bade him farewell.

And of these twelve knights three stayed in those parts[86] and the other nine headed for Portugal, where one of them, who was later the Count of Avranches, did such things in France that he was made Count in that part of Avranches. And this is the Count who met his death at the Alfarrobeira when King Dom Afonso V did battle with Prince Dom Pedro, his uncle and father-in-law. In this battle the aforesaid Prince was also killed. The Prince would say to this Count when he saw so many men on the King's side:

---

86 *in those parts*: From the context it should be understood that three of the knights are now in English-owned territory in France.

"Oh no! Count! What shall we do now?"

And he replied with those immortal words:

"Sire, have lunch here, and then have dinner in Hell!"

Aside from this we do not know what specific deeds he performed in France.

Álvaro de Almada—the one who above is called the Count of Avranches—went to Germany and, in the city of Basel, he fought a great duel with a German. And the agreement was weapon for weapon, kind for kind, on pain of being guilty of treason and never taking up arms again and, like I say, whichever one did not comply being guilty of treason.

These knights entered the enclosure and commenced a frenzied battle against each other that was a wonder to see. And the Portuguese knight having battered the German about, and the German realizing he was by now losing and virtually vanquished, he took a poleaxe that he had brought, and it had a steel hook, and he thrust it at a shoulder and tore off Álvaro de Almada's harness and carried off some flesh from his shoulder on the hook. When Álvaro de Almada saw the hook and how with a single stroke it tore his harness and some of his flesh to pieces, he cast his guisarme to the ground and rushed at the German, grabbing his throat and flinging him to the ground with such fury that his breath left him before he could get up.

And the Emperor, seeing the treachery of the German and how he behaved like a traitor by not complying with the rules according to which they entered the enclosure, declared Álvaro de Almada to be a good knight and the German a traitor.

As for Álvaro Gonçalves, what he did is as follows.

The battle in England now over, Álvaro Gonçalves Magriço traveled to Flanders and made his way to the Count's palace, who was married to Madame Isabel, the daughter of the King of Portugal, Dom João of Happy Memory.

And while he was at his palace the King of France's ambassadors came to see the aforesaid Count of Flanders, and said, on behalf of the King of France, that since the King wished to convene the Courts,[87] he should go to them as was his duty and obligation; at which the Countess was very surprised and she said to the Count:

"Humph! Well! Sire! Are you obliged to go to the Courts of the King of France?"

And he told her that he was, that his father and his forefathers had always upheld that obligation, in compliance of which they went to them whenever they were summoned to do so, and that for this reason he could do nothing else but what they had done because of the obligation that they had. To which she replied that that subjugation saddened her a great deal, and she considered it to be ill fortune, and she considered herself a captive; and she therefore vowed, as the daughter of him of whom she was, that she would free herself of the King of France by not going to his court.

Then the Duke said:

"That, My Lady, cannot be done, for it is happening now because we are descendants, and an end cannot be put to it, by virtue of its being, as it is, a question of the law and the right that the King of France has in this county."

She then said:

"You, My Lord, will not go there, but rather, I shall go."

And, in fulfillment of this vow, she very quickly made preparations and departed for Paris, were the Courts were being held, and she sent for a throne the same as that of the King of France, upon which she sat. And when the princes of France saw her thus, they said: "My Lord, it is not enough that the Count of Flanders does not come to your Courts, but in addition, being your vassal as were all of his forefathers the Dukes of Burgundy, the Duke Dom Philip has ordered a throne for his wife that is the same as yours."

The King then said to the Countess:

---

87 *Courts*: Cp. medieval Portuguese *Côrtes*. These were special meetings of the noble elite convened by the King to discuss and ratify matters of governance and policy.

"And why did the Duke, your husband, not come? Does he not know that the Dukes of his county and duchy of Flanders and Burgundy have always been obliged to attend the Courts?"

To which she replied:

"My Lord, the Duke is not coming because I am appearing here on his behalf, and I say that you have no right to constrain the Duke to come to your Courts, and the reason I am here is that, should you wish that this be determined by force of arms, I shall provide a knight who shall fight one of yours so that the Duke and I and all of our descendants may be free of coming to your Courts ever again, and if your knight vanquishes then the territory will remain obligated as you say, and has been up until now. For when I married the Duke, I did not know of this subjugation that you say I am in, for the daughter of such a great King as I am would not have been allowed to marry a man who is a serf."

When the King of France considered the suit of the Duchess and Countess, which he did because he had in his court very worthy knights in feats of arms who desired no other good than activities in which they could show off their strength, a very valiant French knight immediately stepped forth and begged leave of the King that he grant him that emprise, which the King conceded to him for he knew of his valor and strength in arms. And they then set the deadline that by one month from then she would send her knight so that the two could do battle.

This done, the Duchess returned to Flanders.

Let us leave the quarrels that she had with the King of France about the placement of the throne, how she said that it befitted her for being, as she was, the daughter of such a famous King, and having returned, like I say, to Flanders, she gave an account to the Duke of where the matter stood, and he reprimanded her, saying:

"What was the point of men going to kill each other in a duel?"

Finally, after she sought and besought a great deal, she never found a single Fleming who was willing to accept the challenge, for they believed that she did not have justice on her side. And when the Duchess saw that in Flanders no-one could be found who wished to accept the challenge, she said that Álvaro

Gonçalves Magriço was there, who was the chamberlain of her father the King, and that he would fight on her behalf with the French knight. And when the Duke saw that she was insisting thus, he ordered Álvaro Gonçalves to be called. And when he had come, the Count asked if he wished to enter into that battle on her behalf; and he replied that he did.

And the Duke and Count asked him what he was accustomed to having need of for that type of action, and he said that if the Duke had a friend of some sort at the court of the King of France, whom he trusted to give him what he needed, that he should direct him to him, so that when he was there the friend could provide him with what he had need of; and that for this reason he should give him, as he must, letters to a certain Count, a close friend of Duke Philip, in which he asked him to provide everything necessary, since he was going to clad himself in armor on his behalf, and give him all the best preparation.

With these letters Álvaro Gonçalves departed dressed in the garb of a pilgrim, with his staff in his hand and his clothing fastened, inside of which he carried the letter. And thus, traveling by this route, virtually begging, he came to port at Paris, where the King of France was, along with all of his court, awaiting the deadline so that they could watch the duel.

And as soon as he was in Paris he made his way to the Count's house, and begging for alms he got the Count to come to a window; and The Magriço, realizing that this Count was the one, told him that he wished to give him, as he must, a letter.

And after reading it the Count said to him:

"Are you the knight?"

Álvaro Gonçalves said:

"Sire, I am, and I am dressed in this outfit so that no-one will know who I am."

"By this time tomorrow," said the Count, "The last day of the deadline will have come."

"Aye," said Álvaro Gonçalves, "And I must ask for courtesy's sake, and for all that you owe to the Order of Chivalry, and for the friendship that you have with my lord the Duke, for his being, as he is, a very close friend of yours, that in this act of defiance he sent me expressly to you so that I could rely on you to provide me with an equally reliable armor and horse in order to enter into this duel."

The count replied to him that he would do so, so that, by his own hand, he could break them in. And after sending for some armor and a horse, the count tested it and judged it to be very good, then Álvaro Gonçalves put it on. And riding the horse, being thus very well armed, it was by now late, and there were so many people sitting on the walls and in the stands that it was a wonder.

And the Frenchman, who had been there for twenty-nine days, when it came to the day of the deadline of the duel in which he placed himself and he was riding about well armed, seeing that it was by now very late and that no-one was coming to oppose him, openly and haughtily began to ask out loud for legal instruments about how he found himself there without there being anyone on behalf of Duke Philip who would fight against him.

As this was happening, Álvaro Gonçalves entered into the enclosure, and he began surveying the enclosure and closely inspecting it.

When the Frenchman, who was already in position, saw that the Portuguese knight was spending more time riding around the enclosure, it seemed to him that he was doing so because he was a coward and afraid, and also because he had passed by him two or three times riding right up to the fences without speaking to him, so he said these words out loud to him which were widely overheard:

"I never saw such a ribald knight! And as he shows by his lack of zeal, he must be an aged poltroon for he is avoiding fighting with me so much!"

To which Álvaro Gonçalves replied:

"You, Sir Knight, are lying through your teeth! And for this reason I shall fight you to the death and I shall make you understand that I am a better knight than you."

And both of them charged against each other with great fortitude and made such powerful encounters that, at the same time, both horses and knights fell to the ground, and with great agility they got back up, and they engaged in a combat with swords, which lasted for a very long period of time, not without much admiration from the King and his court.

Finally, Álvaro Gonçalves fought with such fortitude against the Frenchman that at the end of the combat he vanquished him and cut off his head.

And after that he was received by some friends of the Duke and he headed back to him.

And in this way did Álvaro Gonçalves Magriço, at the behest of Madame, free the Count of Flanders from the subjugation of France forever, and great honors and favors were bestowed upon him.

And after that, as he wished to return to Portugal, they wrote to King João of Happy Memory asking him to bestow much honor and favor upon that knight because he had given freedom to the County of Flanders and had delivered it from that subjugation to France; and the King, in recognition of such a great deed, bestowed much favor upon him and made him a Count, and that was the foundation of his own house.

And there is a chronicle in England about these matters, which refers to these knights at length.

Appendix 1

Facsimile of Ms. 87, fols. 260r–265v
Porto, Biblioteca Pública Municipal

The remainder of this page and the following verso page have been intentionally left blank to retain the original recto/verso orientation of the manuscript.

–ed.

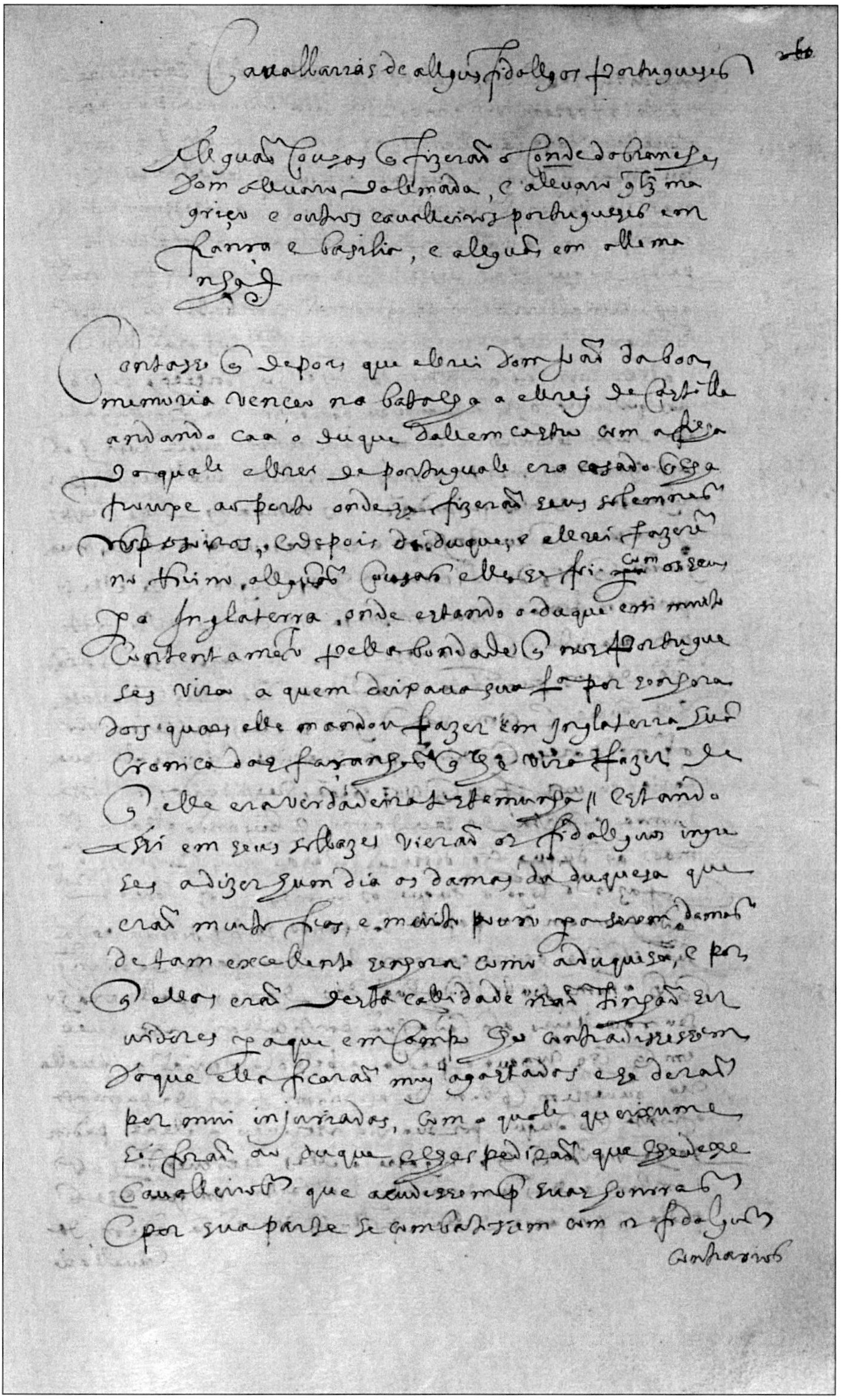

Cavallarias de alguns fidalgos portugueses 260

Alguãs cousas q fizerão o Conde do Brames, Dom Alvaro Dalmada, e Alvaro Gõz Magriço e outros cavalleiros portugueses em França e Basilia, e alguãs em Allemanha.

Contase q depois que elRei dom João da boa memoria venceo na batalha a elRej de Castella andando caa o duque Dalemcastro com a filha do qual elRei de Portugual era casado q esta princepe ao perto ordenarão fizerão seus solemnes desposoiros, e depois do duque e elRei fazerem no fim alguãs cousas elle se foi com os seus pa Inglaterra, onde estando o duque com muito contentamento pella bondade q nos Portugueses vira a quem deixava sua ... por senhora dos quaes elle mandou fazer em Inglaterra sua Cronica das façanhas q lhe vira fazer de q elle era verdadeira testemunha. Estando assi em seus solazes vierão os fidalgos ingleses a dizer hum dia as damas da duquesa que erão muito feas, e muito pouco pera serem damas de tam excellente senhora como a duquesa, e por q ellas erão certo calidade não tinhão servidores q aquelle em campo lho contradisessem, do que ellas ficarão muy agastadas e se derão por mui injuriadas, com o qual queixume se forão ao duque e lhe pedirão que lhes desse cavalleiros que acudissem por suas honras e por sua parte se combatessem com os fidalgos contrarios

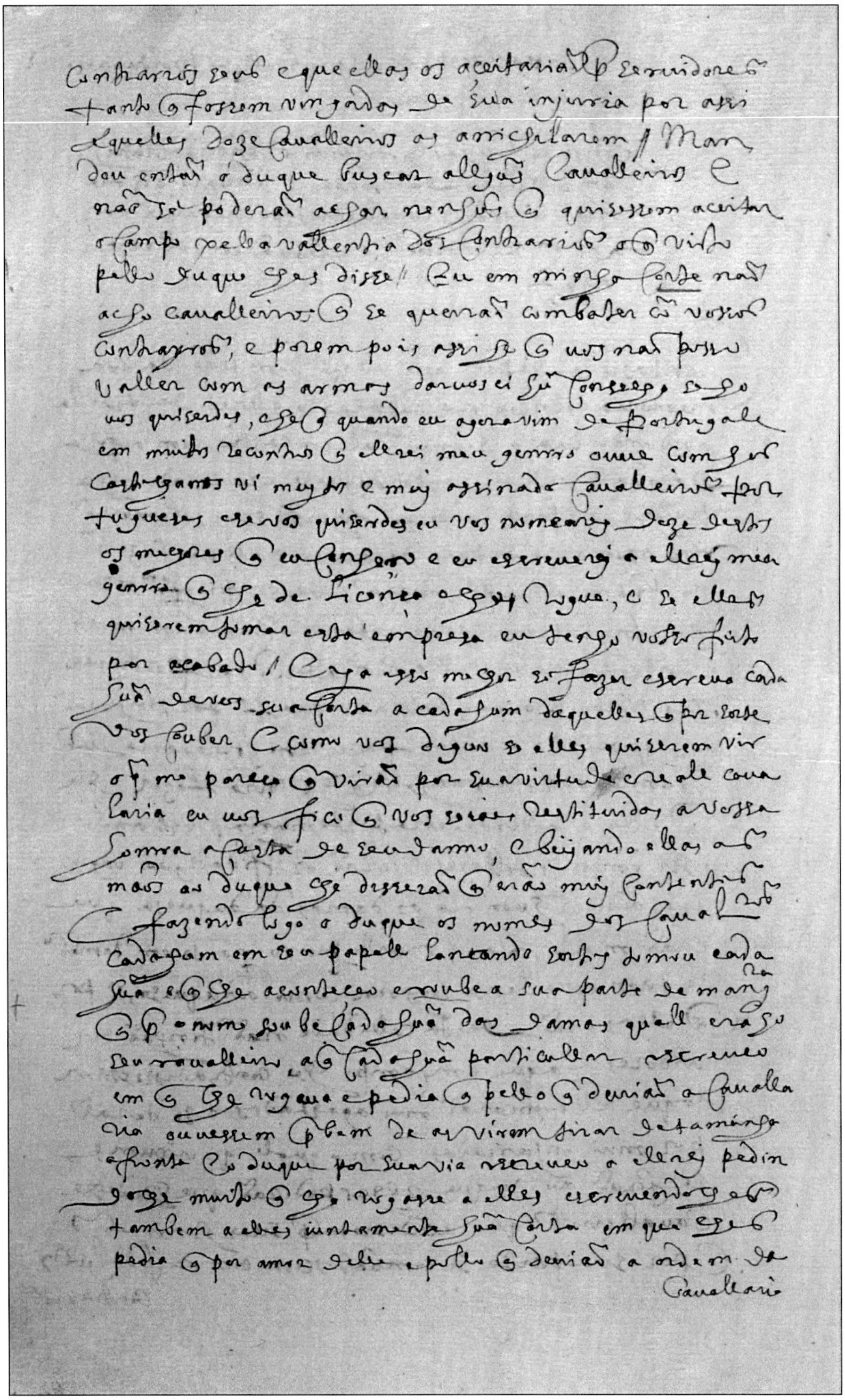

261

Cavallaria quisessem aceitar aquella empresa por cada
hua daquellas damas porque dellas se lhe seguiria grande
honrra fama e louvor por elle não achar em sua parte
cavalleiros q por sua parte dellas o quisessem aceitar // aos
ellas responderão q avida a licença delRei seu senhor
elles serião em Inglaterra o primeiro seguinte que
era o dia do prazo, a qual elle deu logo e elles aos ca
valleiros q se diz serem da serra da estrella da
quelles lugares q estão pella fralda da serra nomo
françes primeiro os quaes cavalleiros erão o 1º
foi conde dabranches em frança e Alvaro dalmada
alvaro glz magriço e Lopo pacheco, e Pedrumem
Coutinho q erão por todos doze todos homes especiaes
em feitos darmas e esprimentados os quaes par
tirão e se forão a cidade do Porto, e se hos onze d
marão hua nao e embarcarão nella e partirão dalli
pera Inglaterra alvaro glz magriço quis hir por terra
desconfiandosse e por ver alguas cousas pello cami
nho prometendolhes q se elle não morresse q elle seria
com elles ao prazo limitado // Partidos os da nao
com prospero vento aportarão na cidade de Londres
onde forão bem recebidos e festeiados das damas e do
duque e a este tempo fallecia mais de dous dias
pa o prazo da batalha e não vinha alvaro glz e da
quam alegres estavão os onze com os seus cavalleiros
tam triste estava aquella a que o dito alvaro glz cou
bera dizendo mal assi q ella era a mais malaventu
rada molher donna de seu cavalleiro e q nella ouvir
de cayir a sorte de não vir e fallecer como se pa
recia pella batalha estar ia tam perto, e estes e
responderão q não se agastasse porque elle era
tal cavalleiro q se morte o não estorvasse elle
virá a tempo q comprisse como o prometera e que
quando aventura quisesse q não viesse q elles
onze se combaterião com os doze ingreses e assi ella
seria

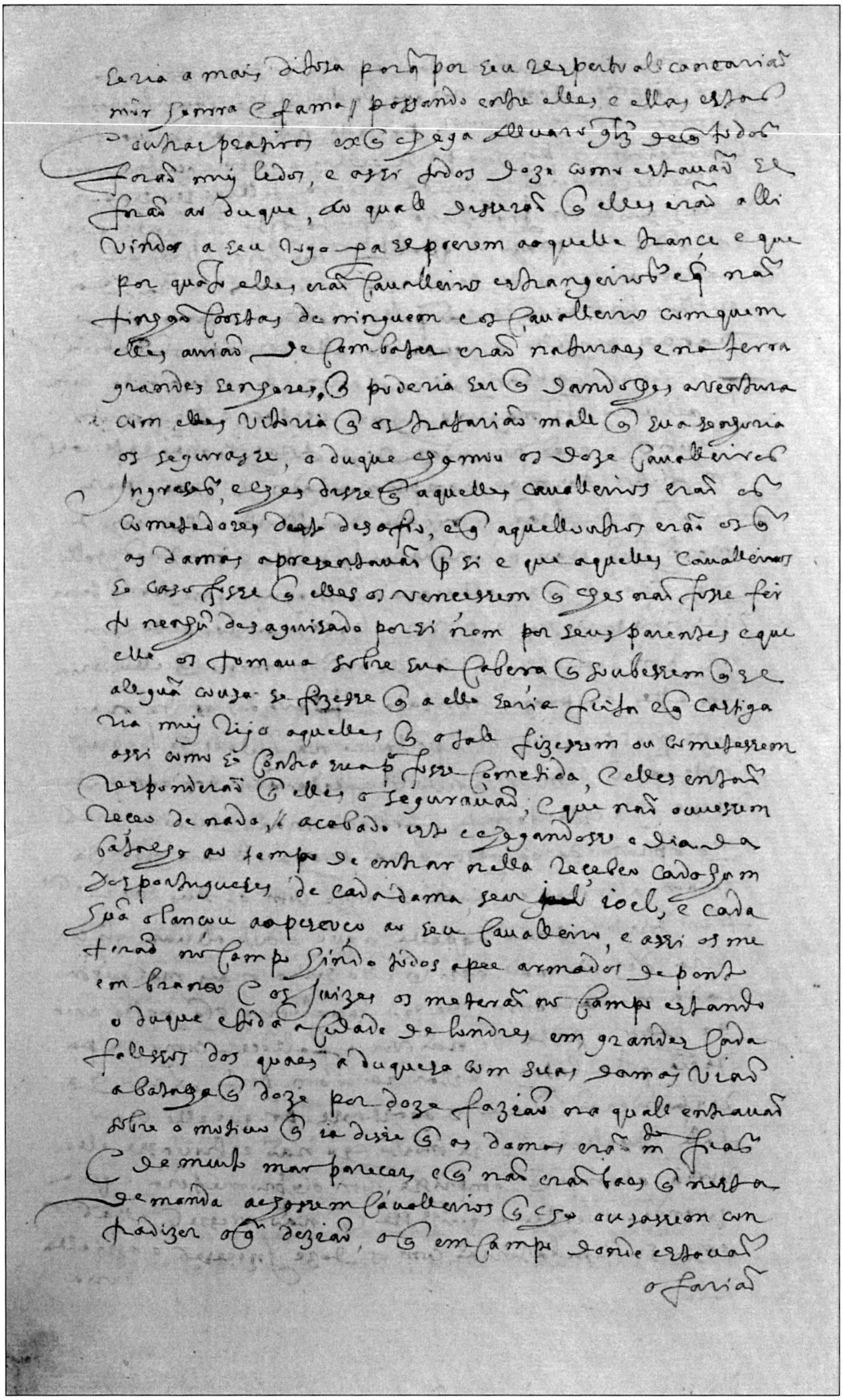

262

o fariaõ conhecer a quem lho contradissesse, a esto
responderaõ os portuguesses q̃ as senhoras eraõ damas
tam gentijs molheres e tam fermosas q̃ por suas gentile
zas mereciaõ q̃ cavalleiros de muj estranhas terras
as viessem servir e morrer q̃ seu serviço com elles
fariaõ se elles lho contradissessem, e sobre estas pa
lavras começaraõ sua batalha com suas maças de
ferro, a qual cometeraõ com tamanho impetu e sanha
q̃ começandose pella manhaã andaraõ todas as horas
da terça por aprazimento de todos se escaramuçaraõ e
acabando de tomar algum tanto repouso tornaraõ a
sua batalha onde os portuguesses meteraõ com com seus
contrarios com tamanho impetu e vigor q̃ finalmente
q̃ ficaraõ os dous delles muj mal e lançando todo fora
do campo ficaraõ elles vencedores e perguntando
aos juizes se tinhaõ mais q̃ fazer pa q̃ aquellas
senhoras fossem restituidas na honra q̃ mereciaõ
q̃ aquelles cavalleiros queriaõ menosprezar elles lhe
disseraõ q̃ naõ, e assi com muita honrra e louvor
se sahiraõ do campo e se foraõ desarmar a sua
casa q̃ para isso estava ordenada onde logo vieraõ
as damas e o duque e ja vedes a allegria q̃ estas
senhoras teriaõ, assentados a mesa pa tomar re
feiçaõ do trabalho passado tomaraõ as damas agua
pa lançarem aas maõs cada hũa a seu cavalleiro
e quando a dama dalvaro glz magriço lhe quis
lançar agoa as maõs elle naõ consentio, e pondo
as maõs de ambas lhe disse senhora nenhũa molher
me lançou agoa as maõs neste mundo e pois isso naõ
consentirej q̃ vos mo façaes, e ella apertando com
elle q̃ o quisesse consentir lhe dixe q̃ pois as ou
tras senhoras o fizeraõ assi cada hũa ao seu cavalleiro
q̃ ella em tida a maõ q̃ a avia de lavrar
o q̃ elle vendo lhe disse // naõ refusava eu a mer
ce

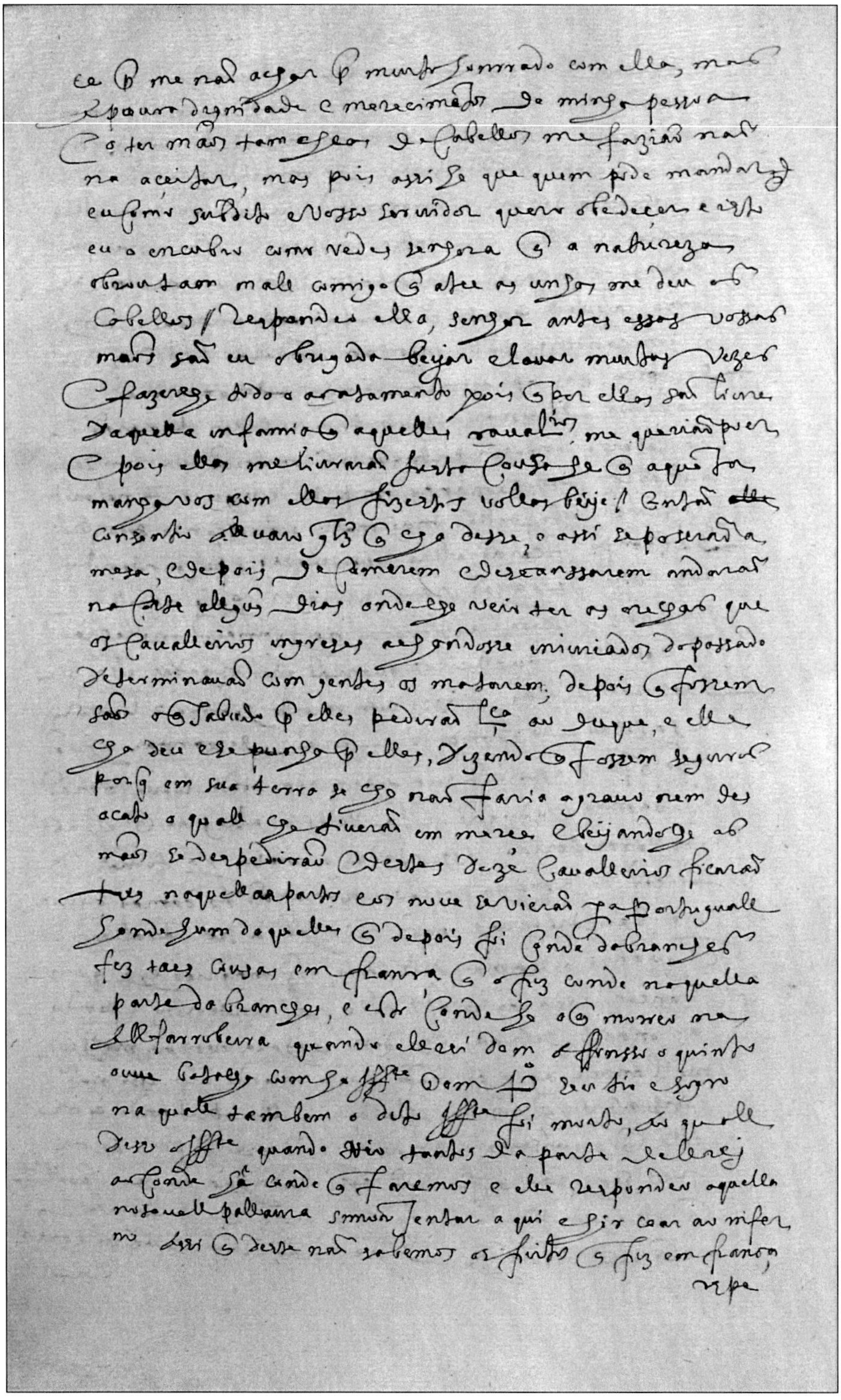
ca q me não aceitar q muito honrrado com ella, mas
a pouca dignidade e merecimento de minha pessoa
e o ter mãos tam feas e cabellos me fazião não
na aceitar, mas pois assi he que quem pode mandar
e a mim subdito e vosso servidor quero obedecer e isto
eu o encubro como vedes senhora q a natureza
obrou tam mal comigo q ate as unhas me deu e os
cabellos / Respondeo ella, senhor antes essas vossas
mãos são eu obrigada beijar e lavar muitas vezes
e fazerlhe todo o agasalhamento pois q por ellas são livre
daquella infamia q aquelles cavaleiros me querião por
e pois ellas me livrarão justo cousa he q aquestas
manos vos com ellas fizestes vollas beije / Então ella
consentio alevanto Sa q o que disse, e assi se posserão a
mesa, e depois de comerem e descansarem andarão
na corte alguns dias onde lhe veio ter os recados que
os cavalleiros ingreses [illegible] iniciados do passado
determinavão com gentes os matarem, depois q forem
sabido o q saberão q elles pedirão lca ao duque, e elle
lha deu e respondeo q elles, dizendo q fossem seguros
porq em sua terra se lhe não faria agravo nem des
acato o qual lhe tiverão em mercê e beijandolhe as
mãos se despedirão e destes doze cavalleiros ficarão
tres naquellas partes e os nove se vierão pa Portugual
e onde hum daquelles q depois foi Conde de Branches
fez taes cousas em França q o fiz conde naquella
parte de Branches, e este Conde he o q morreo na
Alfarrobeira quando el rei dom Afonso o quinto
ouve batalha com o Iffte Dom Po seu tio e sogro
na qual tambem o dito Iffte foi morto, do qual
disse o Iffte quando o vio antes da parte del rei
ao Conde Sr conde q faremos e elle respondeo aquella
notavell pallavra senhor sentar aqui e ir cear ao infer
no assi q deste não sabemos os feitos q fiz em França
Respa

263

espeçificadamente

Alvaro dalmada que foi alemanha e na çidade de [illegible] ouve hum grande desafio com hum alemão, e o conçerto era armas que armas tães que tães sob pena de ser aleivoso e de nunqua mais tomar armas e de ser aleivoso como digo o que não comprisse / e entrarão estes cavaleiros em campo e começarão hua brava batalha entre ambos e era maravilha de ver e trazendo o portugues mal tratado o alemão e vendose perdido e quasi vencido tirou de hum bordão que trazia e ficoulhe hum [illegible] de aceiro e lançoulho a hum ombro e desguarneceo hu arnes a alvaro dalmada e levoulhe [illegible] carne da espadoa quando alvaro dalmada vio o gancho e como da sua vez lhe despedaçara as armas e parte das carnes lançando a bisarma no chão e remetendo a elle com [illegible] apertou a garganta e deu com elle no chão e alli [illegible] primeiro que [illegible] fosse, e vendo o emperador a treição do alemão e como usara de treedor em não comprir os pontos com que entrarão no campo ouve Alvaro dalmada que bem cavaleiro, e ao alemão que treedor.

Quanto a Alvaro gz o que fez he o seguinte. acabada a batalha em Inglaterra Alvaro gz magriço se partiu a frandes e foise a casa do conde, que era casado com madama Isabel que era filha delrei de portugal dom João de boa memoria e andando com sua casa vierão embaixadores delrei de frança pera o dito conde de frandes os quaes dezião da parte delrei de frança que elle queria fazer certo que fosse a elles como devia e era obrigado [illegible] [illegible] muito [illegible] disse ao conde, e bem [illegible] delrei de frança seis vos obrigado de [illegible] e elle

[illegible] de frança

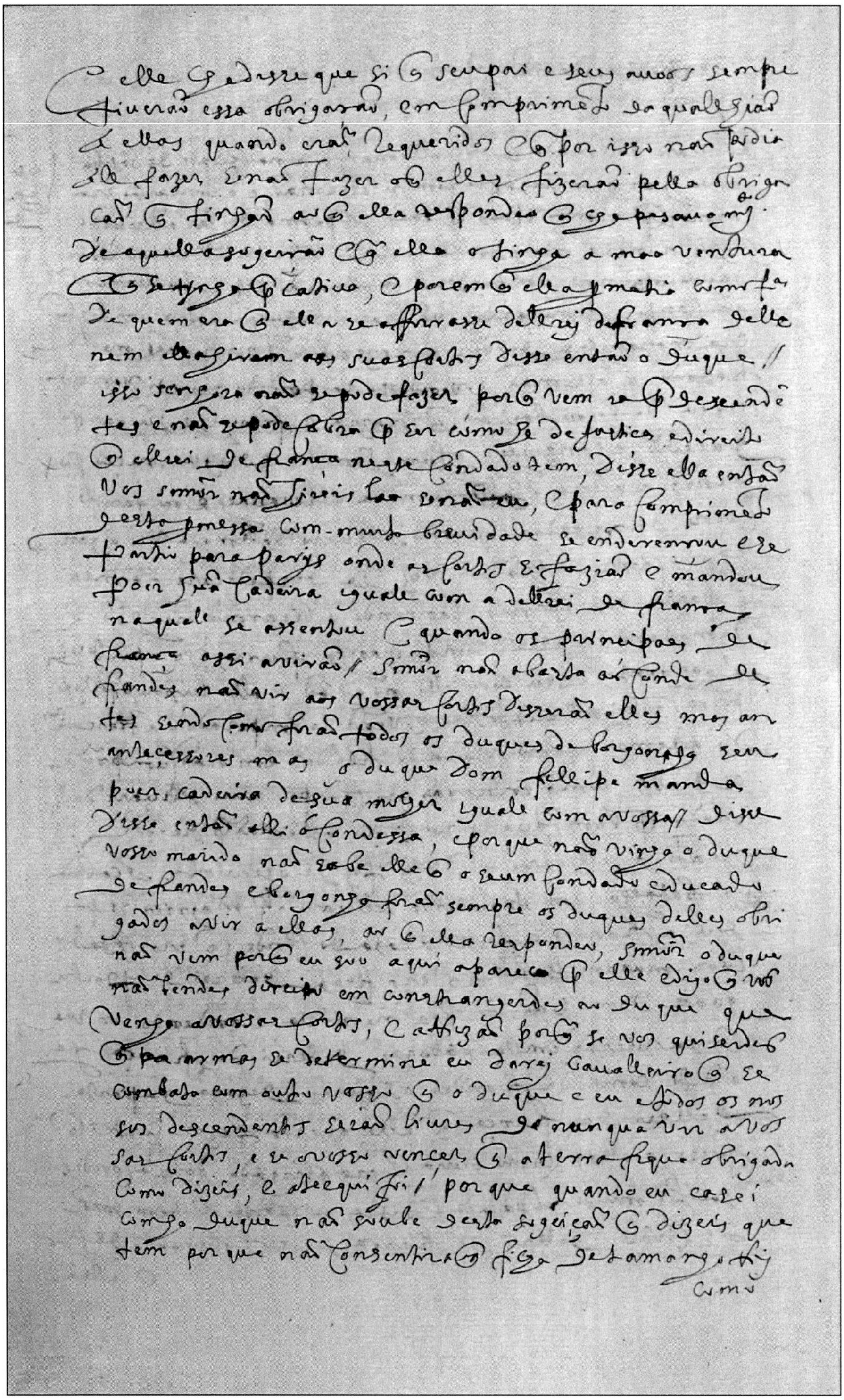

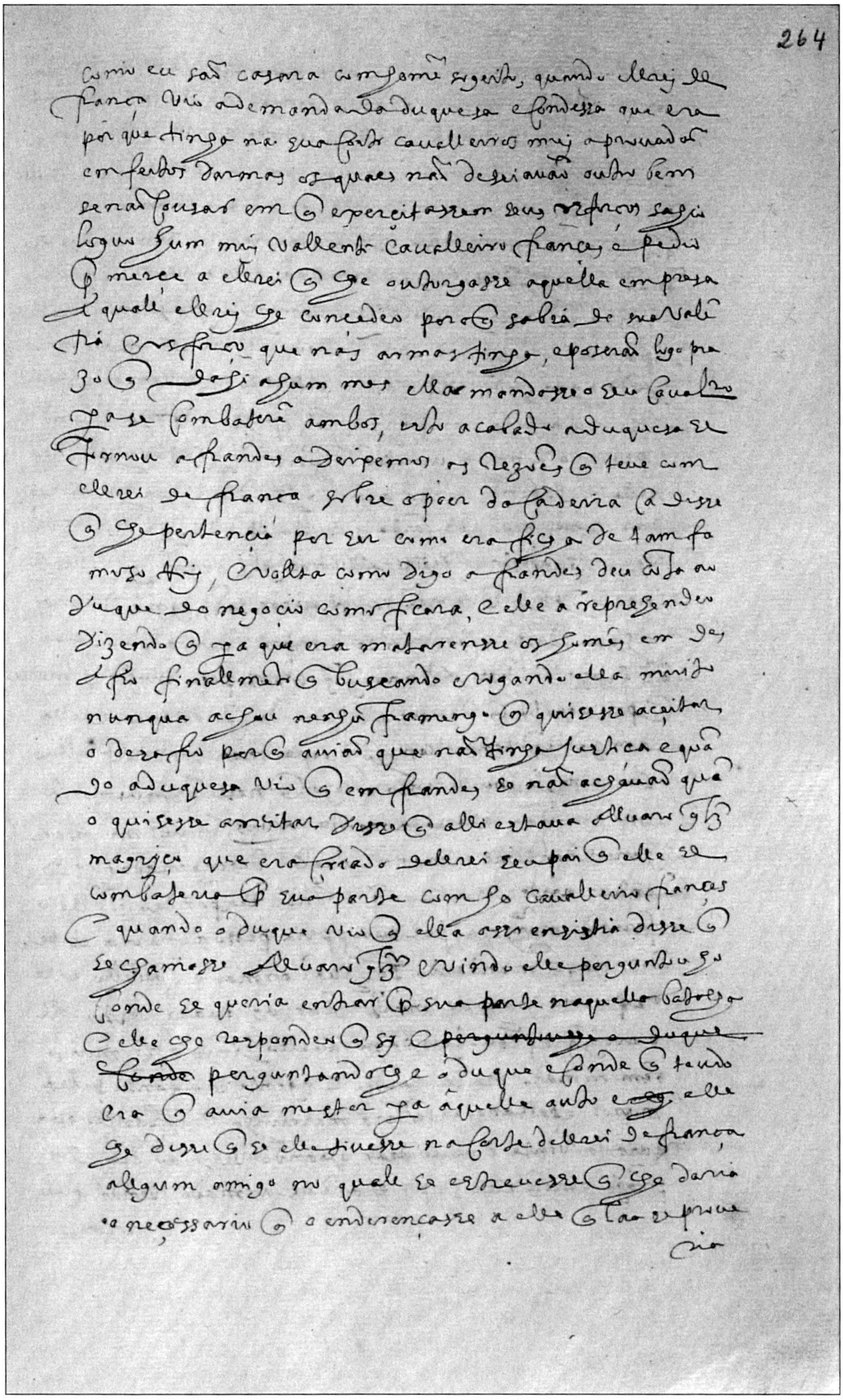
264

como eu sou casada conforme sygerido, quando elrej de
França vio ademandadaduquesa e Condessa que era
porque tinha na sua corte caualleiros muj aprouados
em feitos darmas os quaes nao desejauão outro bem
senão cousas em que exercitassem seus esforços saio
loguo hum muj valente caualleiro frances e pedio
por merce a elrei que lhe outorgasse aquella empresa
a qual elrej lhe concedeo porque sabia de seu vale
tia e esforço que nas armas tinha, e posera logo pra
zo que [illegible] assi a hum mes ella mandasse o seu caualleiro
pera se combaterem ambos, isto acabado a duquesa se
tornou a frandes a [illegible] os rezoes que teue com
elrei de frança sobre o [illegible] a disse
que lhe pertencia por ser como era filha de tam fa
moso Rej, e volta como digo a frandes deu conta ao
duque do negocio como ficara, e elle a reprehendeo
dizendo que ja que era mataremse os homes em de
[illegible] finalmente que buscando e rogando ella muito
nunqua achou nenhum framengo que quisesse aceitar
o desafio porque auião que nao tinha justiça e qua
do a duquesa vio que em frandes se nao achaua quem
o quisesse aceitar disse que alli estaua Aluaro gz
magriço que era criado delrei seu pai que elle se
combateria por sua parte com o caualleiro frances
e quando o duque vio que ella assi ensistia disse que
se chamasse Aluaro gz e vindo elle perguntou-lhe
o onde se queria entrar por sua parte naquella batalha
e elle lhe respondeo que si ~~perguntou-lhe o duque~~
~~donde~~ perguntandolhe o duque e conde que tanto
era que auia mester ja aquelle auto e [illegible] elle
lhe disse que se elle tiuesse na corte delrei de frança
alguum amigo ou quale se escreuesse que lhe daria
o necessario que o encaminhasse a elle que tao [illegible]
cio

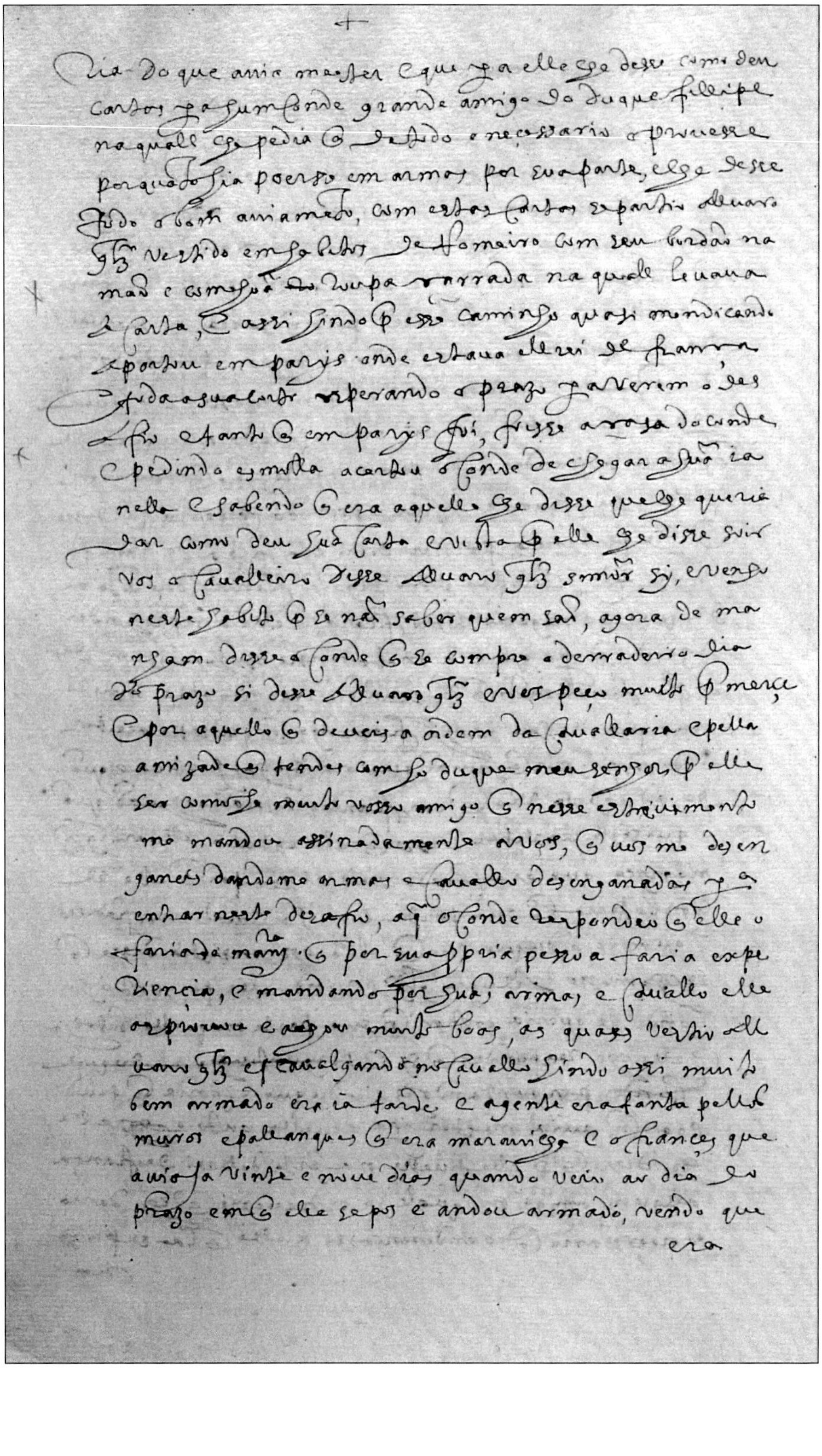

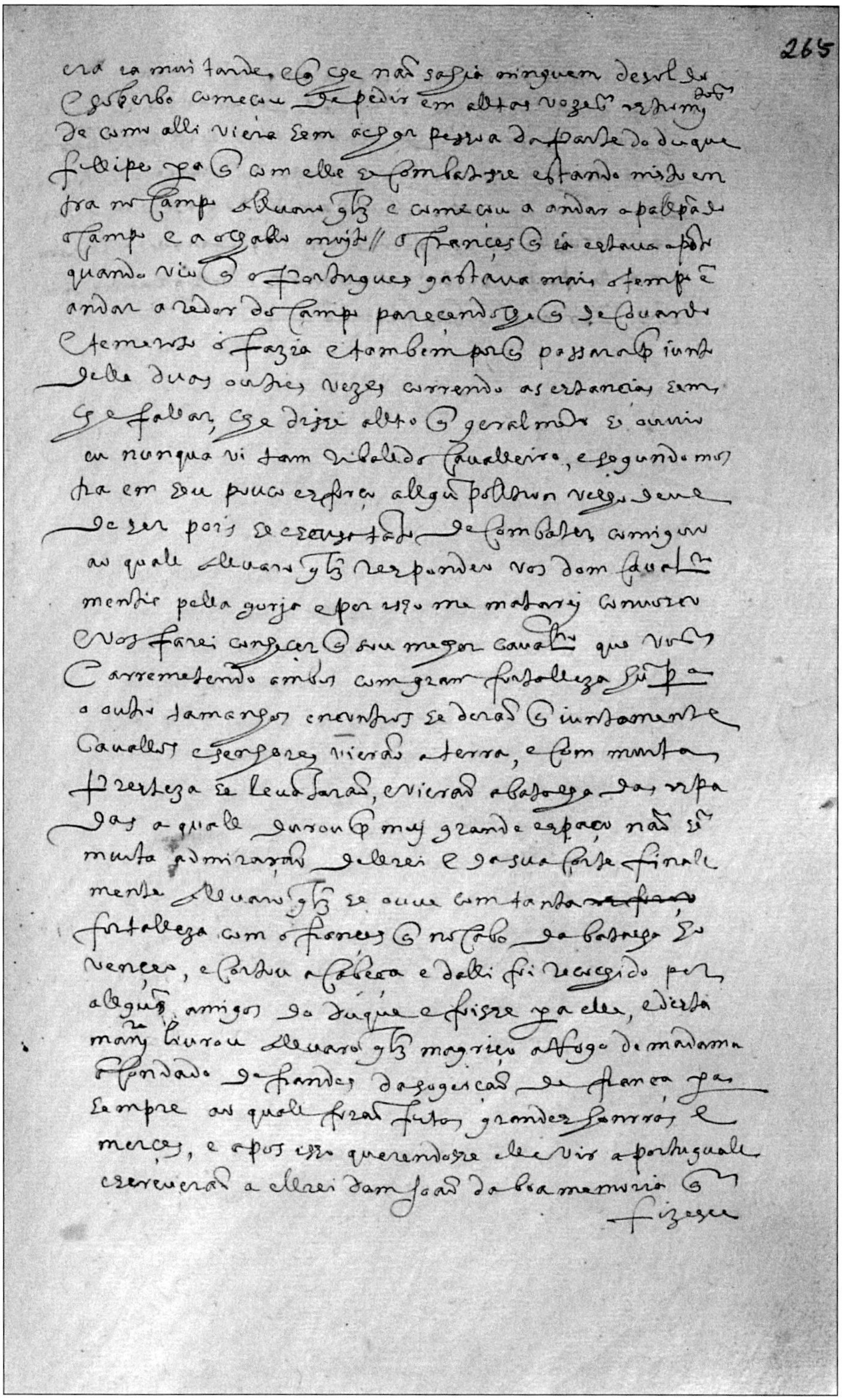
265

era ja mui tarde, e q̃ não sabia ninguem desta[?]
o soberbo começou de pedir em altas vozes ...
de como alli viera sem achar pessoa da parte do duque
fellipe que q̃ com elle se combatesse estando nisto em
tra no campo alvaro glz e começou a andar a passear o
campo e a olhalo muito // o frances que ja estava apos
quando vio q̃ o portugues gastava mais o tempo em
andar a redor do campo parecendo lhe que de covardia
e temor o fazia e tambem porque passara junto
delle duas ou tres vezes correndo as estancias sem
lhe falar, lhe disse alto q̃ geralmente se ouvio
eu nunqua vi tam ... cavaleiro, e segundo mos
tra em seu pouco esforço algũ poltrão velho deve
de ser pois se escusa tanto de combater comigo
ao qual alvaro glz respondeo vos dom eduarte
mentis pella gorja e por isso me matarei comvosco
e vos farei confessar q̃ sou milhor cavalr.º que vos
e arremetendo ambos com gram fortalleza hũ pera
o outro tamanhos encontros se derão q̃ juntamente
cavalos e senhores vierão a terra, e com muita
destreza se levantarão, e vierão a batalha das espa
das a qual durou hũ muy grande espaço não sem
muita admiração delrei e da sua corte finalle
mente alvaro glz se ouve com tanta ~~esforço~~
fortalleza com o frances q̃ no cabo da batalha o
venceo, e cortou a cabeça e dali foi recolhido por
alguns amigos do duque e foisse pera elles, e desta
maneira livrou alvaro glz magriço a honra de madama
e Rondado de frandes da sogeição de frança para
sempre os quais lhe fizerão feitos grandes honras e
merces, e apos isso querendose elle vir a portugualle
escreverão a elrei dom João da boa memoria q̃
fizesse

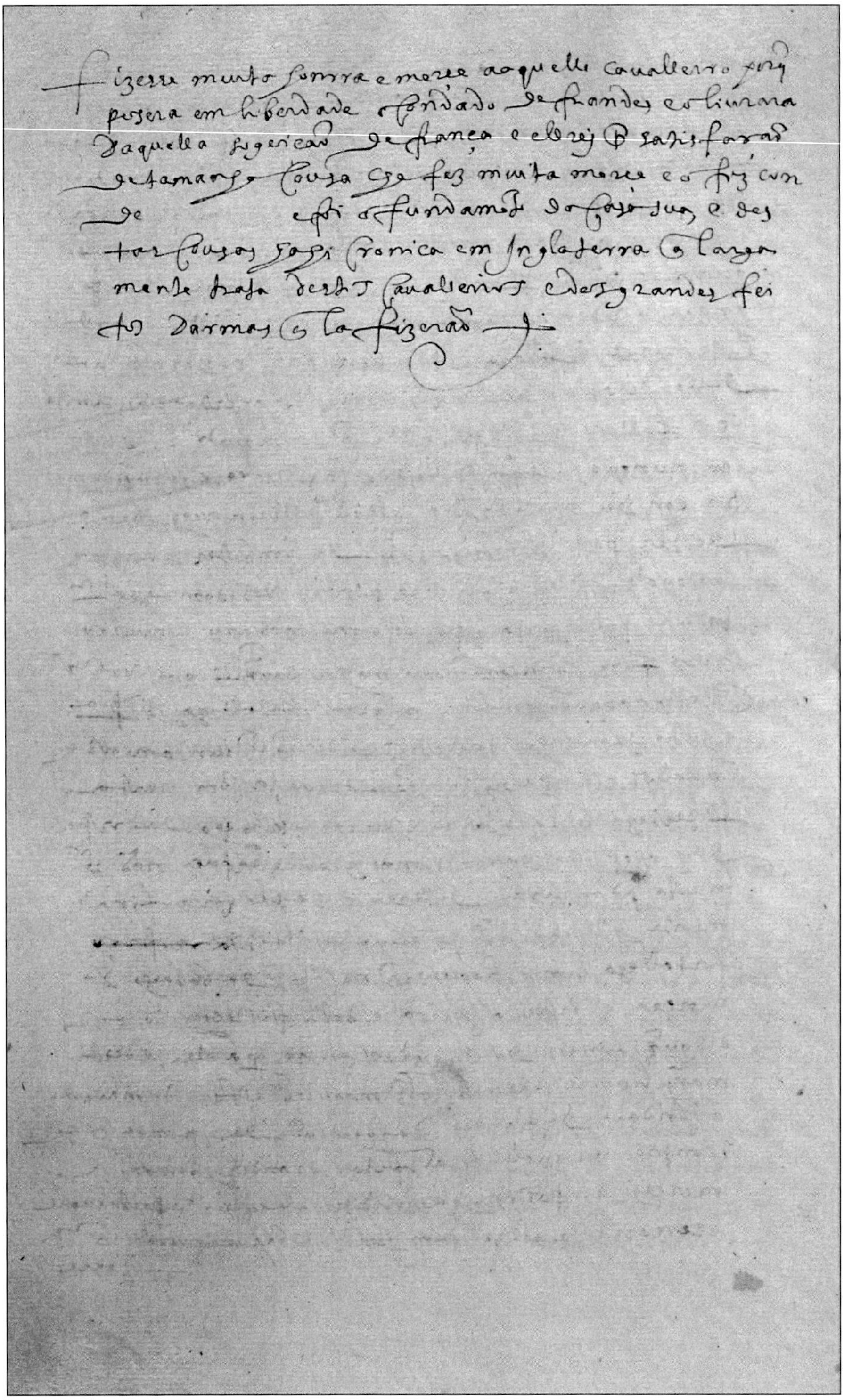
fizerão muito honrra e merçe aquelle cavalleiro porq
posera em liberdade o condado de frandes e o livrara
daquella sugeição de frança e el rej por satisfaraõ
de tamanha cousa q lhe fez muita merce e o fiz com
de este o fundamento do casamento seu, e des
tas cousas faz cronica em inglaterra q larga
mente trata destes cavaleiros e dos grandes fei
tos darmas q la fizeraõ.

Appendix 2

Genealogical Tables

I. Portugal and Burgundy

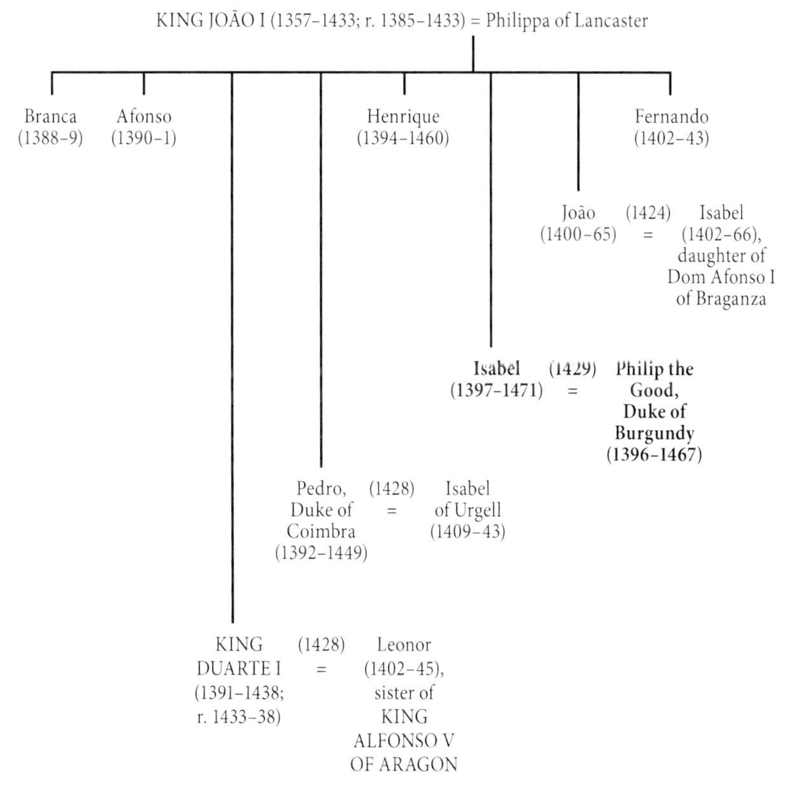

II. The House of Lancaster and the Royal Houses of Portugal and Castile

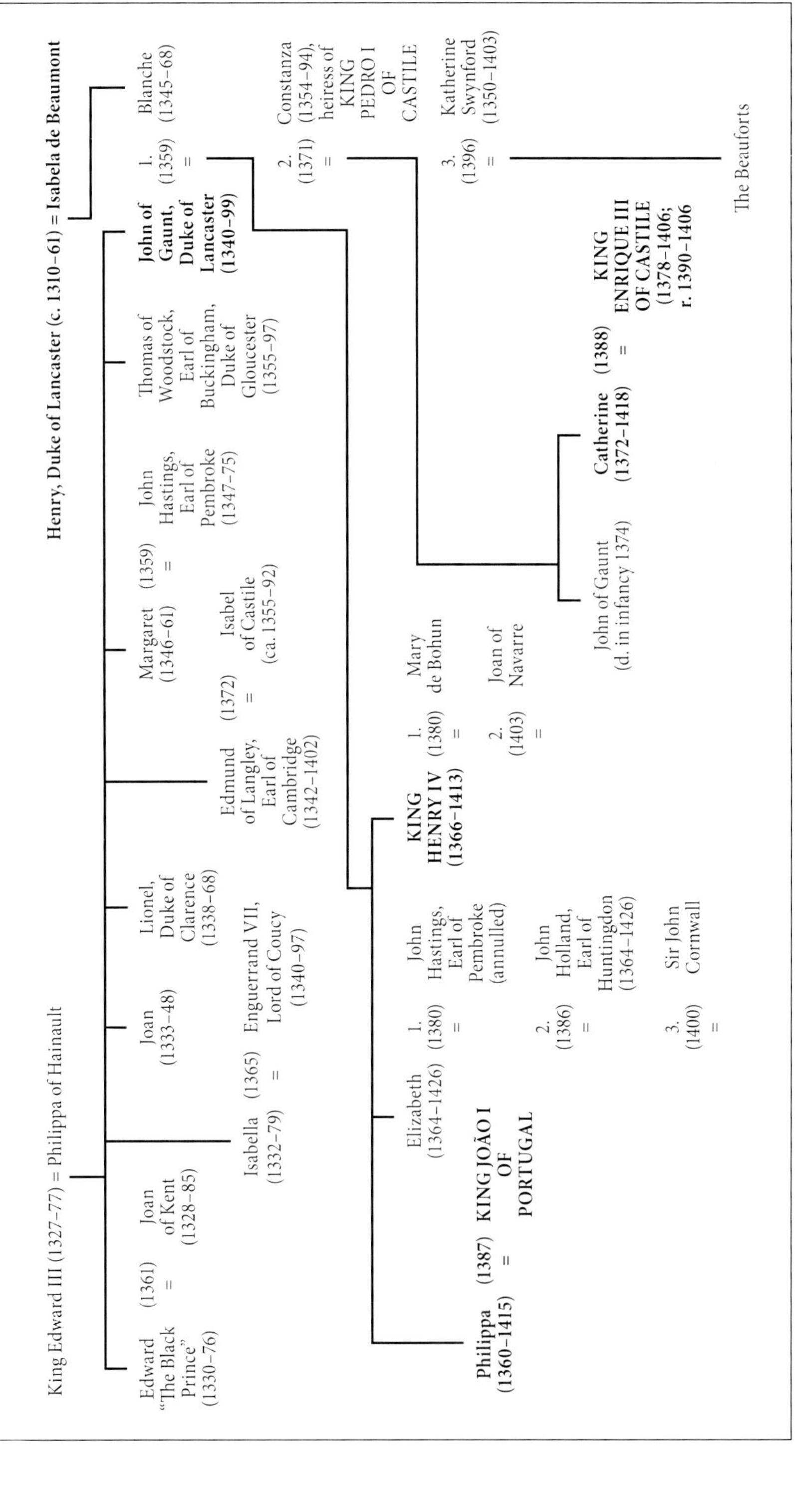

Appendix 3

Maps

Europe in the Fifteenth Century

FRANCE AND BURGUNDY IN THE FIFTEENTH CENTURY

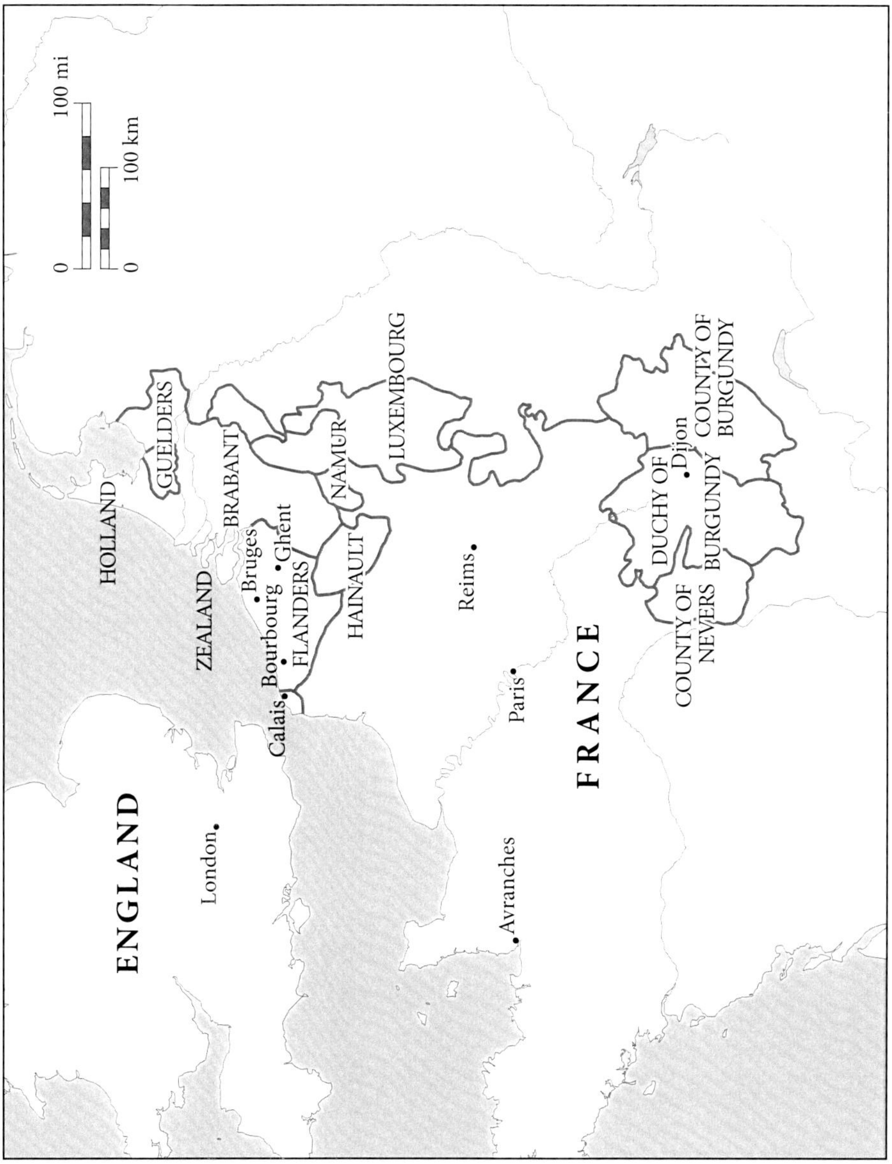

THE IBERIAN PENINSULA IN THE FIFTEENTH CENTURY

Bibliography

Manuscript

Porto, Biblioteca Pública Municipal, Ms. 87, fols. 260r–265v.

Printed Works

Alfonso X, King of Castile. *Las Siete Partidas*, trans. Samuel Parsons Scott and Robert I. Burns, S.J. 5 vols. Philadelphia: University of Pennsylvania Press, 2001.

Anglo, Sydney. "*Le Jeu de la Hache*: A 15th-Century Treatise on the Technique of Chivalric Axe Combat." In *Masters of Medieval and Renaissance Martial Arts. Rediscovering the Western Combat Heritage*, ed. John Clements. Boulder: Paladin Press, 2008. 143–71.

———. *The Martial Arts of Renaissance Europe*. New Haven: Yale University Press, 2000.

Baquero Moreno, Humberto. *A Batalha de Alfarrobeira. Antecedentes e significado histórico*. 2 vols. Coimbra: Imprensa de Coimbra, 1979–80.

BITAGAP: Bibliografia de Textos Antigos Galegos e Portugueses http://sunsite.berkeley.edu/Philobiblon/phhmbp.html (2012).

Blair, Claude, Ian Eaves and Carlo Paggiarino. *Historic Armour and Arms in the Castle of Churburg.* Milan: Hans Prunner Editore, 2006.

Camões, Luis Vaz de. *The Lusíads*, trans. Landeg White. Oxford: Oxford University Press, 1997.

Capwell, Tobias. *The Real Fighting Stuff. Arms and Armour at Glasgow Museums.* Glasgow: Glasgow City Council, 2007.

———. *The Wallace Collection. The Complete Digital Catalogue of European Arms and Armour.* London: Paul Holberton, 2011.

Ceballos-Escalera y Gila, Alfonso. *La Orden y Divisa de la Banda Real de Castilla*. Madrid: Prensa y Ediciones Iberoamericanas, 1993.

Coelho, Maria Helena da Cruz. *D. João I, o que re-colheu "Boa Memória."* Lisbon: Temas e Debates, Círculo de Leitores, Centro de Estudos dos Povos e Culturas de Expressão Portuguesa, 2008.

Correa, Manoel. *Os Lusíadas do grande Luis de Camõens; Principe da poesia heroica. Commentados pelo Licenciado Manoel Correa, Examinador Synodal do Arcebispado de Lisboa & Cura da Igreja de S. Sebastião da Mouraria, natural da cidade de Elvas.* Lisbon: Pedro Crasbeeck, 1613. [Available at books.google.com]

DeVries, Kelly, and Robert Douglas Smith, *Medieval Military Technology,* 2nd ed. Toronto: University of Toronto Press, 2012.

Dias Arnaut, Salvador. *A Batalha de Trancoso.* Coimbra: Faculdade de Letras da Universidade de Coimbra, 1947.

Duarte I, King of Portugal. *The Art of Riding on Every Saddle*, trans. António Franco Preto and Luís Preto. Lexington: CreateSpace, 2011.

Eschenbach, Wolfram von. *Parzival*, trans. A.T. Hatto. Harmondsworth: Penguin, 1980.

Fallows, Noel. *Jousting in Medieval and Renaissance Iberia*. Woodbridge: Boydell, 2010.

Faria e Sousa, Manuel de. *Lusíadas de Luis de Camões. Comentadas por Manuel de Faria e Sousa. Reprodução fac-similada pela edição de 1639*, ed. Jorge de Sena. 2 vols. Lisbon: Imprensa Nacional-Casa da Moeda, 1972.

Ferreira de Vasconcellos, Jorge. *Memorial das proezas da Segunda Tavola Redonda*, 2nd ed. Lisbon: Typ. do Panorama, 1867. [Available at books.google.com]

France, Marie de. *The Lais of Marie de France*, trans. Glyn S. Burgess and Keith Busby. Harmondsworth: Penguin, 1986.

Goodman, Anthony. *John of Gaunt. The Exercise of Princely Power in Fourteenth-Century Europe.* Harlow: Longman, 1992.

Guerreau-Jalabert, Anita. *Index des Motifs Narratifs dans les Romans Arthuriens français en vers (XIIe–XIIIe siècles) [Motif-Index of French Arthurian Verse Romances (XIIth–XIIIth cent.)].* Geneva: Droz, 1992.

Harney, Michael. "Amadís, Superhero," *La corónica* 40.2 (2012): 291–318.

Hutchinson, Amélia P. "Anglo-Portuguese Relations and Arthurian Revival in Portugal." In *Actas do Colóquio Comemorativo do VI Centenário do Tratado de Windsor (de 15 a 18 de Outubro de 1986)*, ed. M. Gomes da Torre, Rui Carvalho Homem, Maria Teresa Castilho, and Belinda Sousa Maia. Porto: Faculdade de Letras do Porto, 1988. 275–88.

———. "*Os Doze de Inglaterra*: A Romance of Anglo-Portuguese Relations in the Later Middle Ages?" In *England and Iberia in the Middle Ages, 12th–15th Century*, ed. María Bullón-Fernández. New York: Palgrave Macmillan, 2007. 167–87.

Jager, Eric. *The Last Duel. A True Story of Crime, Scandal, and Trial by Combat in Medieval France.* New York: Broadway Books, 2004.

Joubert, Felix. *Catalogue of the Collection of European Arms & Armour Formed at Greenock by R.L. Scott*, ed. Robert C. Woosnam-Savage and Tobias Capwell. Huntingdon: Ken Trotman Publishing, 2006.

LaRocca, Donald J. "Afonso 'the African' and his Army: The Pastrana Tapestries as a Visual Encyclopedia for the Study of Arms and Armor." In *The Invention of Glory: Afonso V and the Pastrana Tapestries.* Madrid: Ediciones el Viso, 2011. 29–41.

Latin Arthurian Literature, ed. and trans. Mildred Leake Day. Cambridge: D.S. Brewer, 2005.

Lopes, Fernão. *Crónica de D. João I*, ed. António Sérgio. 2 vols. Porto: Livraria Civilização, 1945–9.

———. *The English in Portugal 1367–87. Extracts from the Chronicles of Dom Fernando and Dom João*, ed. and trans. Derek W. Lomax and R.J. Oakley. Warminster: Aris & Phillips Ltd., 1988.

MacKay, Angus. *Spain in the Middle Ages. From Frontier to Empire, 1000–1500.* London: Macmillan, 1977.

Magalhães Basto, Artur de. *O essencial sobre Os Doze de Inglaterra.* Lisbon: Imprensa Nacional-Casa da Moeda, 1986.

——— and Joaquim Costa. *Relação ou Crónica breve das cavalarias dos Doze de Inglaterra (Ms. quinhentista da Biblioteca Pública Municipal do Pôrto).* Porto: Imprenta Portuguesa, 1935.

Mann, Sir James. *Wallace Collection Catalogues. European Arms and Armour: Text with Historical Notes and Illustrations.* 2 vols. London: William Clowes and Sons Ltd., 1962.

Marche, Olivier de la. *Mémoires d'Olivier de la Marche, maître d'hôtel et capitaine des gardes de Charles le Téméraire*, ed. Henri Beaune and J. D'Arbaumont. 4 vols. (Société de l'Histoire de France – Publications, nos. 213, 219, 220, 240). Paris: Librairie Renouard, 1883–8.

Mariz, Pedro de. *Dialogos de varia historia: em que sumariamente se referem muytas cousas antiguas de Hespanha.* Coimbra: Antonio de Mariz, 1598. [Available at books.google.com]

Martorell, Joanot. *Tirant lo Blanc. The Complete Translation*, trans. Ray LaFontaine. New York: Peter Lang, 1993.

Menezes, Fernando de, Conde da Ericeira. *Vida e Acçõens d'el Rey Dom João I*. Lisbon: Na Officina de João Galrão, 1677. [London, British Library, shelfmark 10632.aaa.19]

Miller, Barbara D. "Hispanic Arthurian Literature." In *A History of Arthurian Scholarship*, ed. Norris J. Lacy. Cambridge: D.S. Brewer, 2006. 179–89.

Mondschein, Ken. *The Knightly Art of Battle*. Los Angeles: Getty Publications, 2011.

Monteiro, João Gouveia. *Aljubarrota 1385. A Batalha Real*. Lisbon: Tribuna da História, 2003.

Muhlberger, Steven. *Deeds of Arms. Formal Combats in the Late Fourteenth Century*. Highland Village: Chivalry Bookshelf, 2005.

———. *Jousts and Tournaments. Charny and the Rules for Chivalric Sport in Fourteenth-Century France*. Union City: Chivalry Bookshelf, 2002.

Nadot, Sébastien. *Le Spectacle des joutes. Sport et courtoisie à la fin du Moyen Âge*. Rennes: Presses Universitaires de Rennes, 2012.

Neste, Évelyne van den. *Tournois, joutes, pas d'armes dans les villes de Flandre à la fin du Moyen Âge (1300–1486)*. Paris: École des Chartes, 1996.

Norman, A.V.B. *Wallace Collection Catalogues. European Arms and Armour: Supplement*. London: Balding and Mansell Ltd., 1986.

O'Callaghan, Joseph F. *A History of Medieval Spain*. Ithaca: Cornell University Press, 1990.

Oliveira, Luís Filipe. *A Casa dos Coutinhos. Linhagem, Espaço e Poder (1360–1452)*. Cascais: Patrimonia Historica, 1999.

Palmer, John, and Brian Powell. *The Treaty of Bayonne (1388) with preliminary Treaties of Trancoso (1387)*. Exeter Hispanic Texts XLVII. Exeter: Exeter University Press, 1988.

Reverseau, Jean-Pierre. "L'Habit de guerre des français en 1446. Le manuscrit anonyme fr. 1997 de la Bibliothèque Nationale," *Gazette des Beaux-Arts*, Series 6, 93 (1979): 179–98.

Riley, Carlos Guilherme. *Os Doze de Inglaterra: Ficção e Realidade*. Unpublished Ph.D. dissertation. Ponta Delgada: University of the Azores, 1988.

——— and Ana Maria S.A. Rodrigues. "Les Joutes d'Alvaro Gonçalves Coutinho à Paris: Un épisode portugais au conflit entre les maisons de Valois et de Bourgogne." In *Théâtre et spectacles hier et aujourd'hui: Moyen Âge et Renaissance (Actes du 115e Congrès National des Sociétés Savantes, Avignon 1990)*. Paris: Éditions du CTHS, 1991. 305–19.

Rodrigues Védouro, Ignacio. *Desafio dos doze de Inglaterra, que na corte de Londres se combateram em desaggravo das damas inglezas*. Lisbon: Na Officina Ferreiriana, 1732. [London, British Library, shelfmark 9195.c.36]

Rodríguez Velasco, Jesús D. *Order and Chivalry. Knighthood and Citizenship in Late Medieval Castile*, trans. Eunice Rodríguez Ferguson. Philadelphia: University of Pennsylvania Press, 2010.

Ruiz, Teófilo F. *A King Travels. Festive Traditions in Late Medieval and Early Modern Spain*. Princeton: Princeton University Press, 2012.

Russell, P.E. *The English Intervention in Spain & Portugal in the Time of Edward III & Richard II*. Oxford: Clarendon Press, 1955.

Santos, J.J. Moreira dos. "O Medievalismo en Camões. Os Doze de Inglaterra," *Revista da Universidade de Coimbra* 33 (1985): 209–20.

Soares da Silva, José. *Memórias para a Historia de Portugal que comprehendem o governo del rey D. João o I: do anno 1383 até o anno de 1433*. 4 vols. Lisbon: Joseph Antonio da Silva, 1730–34. [Available at books.google.com]

Soeiro, Manuel. *Los Anales de Flandes*. 2 vols. Antwerp: Pedro and Juan Belleros, 1624. [Available at books.google.com]

Sommé, Monique. *Isabelle de Portugal, duchesse de Bourgogne. Une femme au pouvoir au XVe siècle*. Villeneuve d'Ascq (Nord): Presses Universitaires du Septentrion, 1998.

Stevens, John. *Medieval Romance. Themes and Approaches*. London: Hutchinson University Library, 1973.

Taylor, Aline S. *Isabel of Burgundy. The Duchess Who Played Politics in the Age of Joan of Arc, 1397–1471*. Lanham: Madison Books, 2001.

Trapp, Oswald Graf, with Mario Scalini, Rudolf H. Wackernagel and Ian Eaves. *The Armoury of the Castle of Churburg*. 2 vols. Udine: Magnus Edizioni, 1996.

Troyes, Chrétien de. *Arthurian Romances*, trans. D.D.R. Owen. London: Everyman, 1996.

Vargas Díaz-Toledo, Aurelio. "A literatura cavaleiresca portuguesa: estado da questão." In *De cavaleiros e cavalarias. Por terras de Europa e Américas*, ed. Lênia Márcia Mongelli. São Paulo: Humanitas, 2012. 146–56.

Waldman, John. *Hafted Weapons in Medieval and Renaissance Europe. The Evolution of European Staff Weapons between 1200 and 1650*. Leiden: Brill, 2005.

Ward, Renée. "To Be a 'Fleschhewere': Beheading, Butcher-Knights, and Blood Taboos in *Octavian Imperator*." In *Heads Will Roll. Decapitation in the Medieval and Early Modern Imagination*, ed. Larissa Tracy and Jeff Massey. Leiden: Brill, 2012. 159–81.

Woosnam-Savage, Robert. "The 'AVANT' Armour and R.L. Scott," *The Park Lane Arms Fair* 7 (1990): 5–11.